JOYFUL
SELLING

JOYFUL SELLING

A BETTER WAY TO YES
for Heart-Centered Coaches

MICHELLE ROCKWOOD

LIONCREST
PUBLISHING

JOYFUL SELLING
A Better Way to Yes for Heart-Centered Coaches

ISBN   978-1-5445-3174-8   *Hardcover*

       978-1-5445-3173-1   *Paperback*

       978-1-5445-3172-4   *Ebook*

CONTENTS

For heart-centered coaches everywhere.

INTRODUCTION

I HAVE A SUPERPOWER.

As soon as someone says "hello," I know whether or not we're going to work together.

I wasn't born with this ability; this superpower has developed over time. I've discovered that "hello" sets the tone and reveals possibility. It creates a feeling in my body that overcomes me. That single word releases a specific energy, and I open my heart even further to receive.

When I hear that "hello," I settle in, excited to serve and support the person in front of me. My focus and intention is to help them figure out the choice they need to make and the impact it will have on their life.

This interaction is likely a far cry from the sales methods you're familiar with. You know, make seven calls to obtain one client. Follow up relentlessly to get a yes at all costs. These traditional methods of selling focus on quantity over quality, and they don't work when it comes to enrolling people in coaching programs. These methods aren't heart-centered, meaning they don't serve the client, and they most certainly don't serve *you*.

THE PROBLEM WITH TRADITIONAL SALES

If you've been using traditional sales methods to try and sell your coaching, you've likely encountered some problems. Do any of these sound familiar?

- There aren't enough hours in the day for you to do your work. Finding clients, scheduling sales calls, hosting follow-ups, and then delivering your coaching is just too much!

- You don't have enough dollars in the bank to market yourself. Without money to spend on paid ads, you're left fishing for clients on social media, hoping and praying for a bite.

- You're not a salesperson. You know you have to "sell," but you got into this job to help people, not to chase or convince.

- Your inbox is filled with "maybes," leaving you unsure of your next step.

- Sales calls leave you feeling drained because you feel like you're manipulating prospective clients. When you're not 100 percent in your integrity, you feel deeply unsettled and exhausted.

- You're heartbroken because what you have to offer can change the world, but you haven't been able to share it. You need to find the words so you can create an impact.

- You enjoy your successes, but they are confusing. It's not clear why some prospects join, and others don't, leaving you stuck in a loop of feast or famine.

- You enroll misaligned clients. This leaves you feeling drained, which leads you to question your coaching ability and your desire to continue your life's work.

If you've been using traditional sales methods and can identify with any of these struggles, it's time to make a change.

It's time to work from your heart center.

THE BENEFITS OF HEART-CENTERED SALES

Conducting heart-centered business in coaching programs begins with the word "hello." Your success, and the success of the individual if they become your client, all begin with that simple word. On a sales call, that one word lets you know if the client is embodied and engaged. It lets you know if they're invested and willing to focus.

Heart-centered sales also means that you will no longer want or need to mass market yourself. You won't have to go all out like you're Coca-Cola or one of the Kardashians. You'll be working face-to-face with clients and prospective clients, have embodied conversations, and create a client-coach partnership. All of this happens person-to-person, not en masse or through a social media campaign. With heart-centered sales, you can also charge more, which means you can enroll fewer clients. And *that* means you can give each person you work with the care and attention they deserve, without stressing about your income.

BREAKING AWAY FROM THE PAST

I have to confess that I didn't always practice heart-centered sales. After graduating from college, I moved to Southern California and sold real estate. The culture was rife with networking and BS, and I had to lay down my life for prospective clients. I took calls at night and scheduled showings at any hour of the day. I always had to be available, no matter what.

In that crazy sales environment, it was often every woman for herself, but I eventually elbowed my way into some high-priced listings. I vividly remember getting my first commission check for a cool $20,000.

Since I made my money through networking and BS, naturally I thought I should spend my commission on something that would take all of it to the next level. I wanted to project an image, appearing to be wealthier than I really was, so I used that $20,000 to make a down payment on a Mercedes.

And you know what? Driving my Mercedes and continuing the facade actually worked, and I made great money. But there was one major problem for this tree-hugging girl: I felt awful. I was using sales methods that were completely contradictory to my core values, and it was getting to me.

I began to experience a severe disconnect between what I was doing and what I truly wanted in life. I loved sales, but I had a desire for deep, meaningful, authentic relationships. I wanted to serve people—I mean *really* serve them. And I couldn't do that by continuing down the path I was on.

I knew I had more to offer, so I quit. I ran away. I truly, literally ran away. I joined the Peace Corps and headed to Mali in West Africa.

THE TURNAROUND

From selling properties in one of the wealthiest communities in Southern California to sleeping on a dirt floor in Mali, I experienced two extremes of the financial spectrum, and I learned valuable lessons from both. In California, I learned what it was like to receive generous financial compensation for my work. In Mali, I learned what it felt like to truly serve.

My two experiences brought to light the fact that our society has not only inappropriately defined sales and success; it's also inappropriately defined what service looks like. When we think of the ultimate servant, we picture Jesus or Mother Teresa. We think the epitome of serving is being destitute and broke, always putting the needs of others above our own. None of this is accurate—there are many ways to serve without starving yourself.

I returned to the United States after serving in Mali for one year. I started my career again in Youngstown, Ohio. This time, I did fundraising for nonprofit organizations. I raised money for a shelter that helped homeless women and children. Then I moved to Cleveland and worked for one of the biggest health care institutions in the United States, raising money for their heart and vascular team.

This job was unique—I flew around the country and met with potential donors in their living rooms. Back in those days we didn't have the option for video conferencing, and I had never met most of the donors in person before, but they always welcomed me in. I got uniquely comfortable asking intimate questions about their deepest desires and greatest fears. And I got really comfortable talking about money!

While I was incredibly successful at this job and enjoyed connecting with others, something was still missing. That something was *me*.

This job didn't allow me to receive in a way that was equal to my talents and contributions. And when you constantly give and don't receive, you feel taken advantage of. The work isn't sustainable, nor is it rewarding or inspiring. Every human being has an innate need to have all their buckets filled, and some of mine were empty.

Through a series of other events and realizing my need to receive, I was eventually able to start a coaching business and marry my two loves: sales and service. Through experience, I was able to view sales through a different lens, and embrace new, heart-centered methods that I will share with you in this book.

FILL (ALL) YOUR BUCKETS

Before you continue to read, I want to make it clear that this book isn't for everyone. It's not for those who are selling tangible goods, like books, trinkets, or toilet plungers. This book is for people who coach, interact, and build relationships. It's for people who care about their energy and how they feel day-to-day. It's for those who know they need to make money and want to feel good about *how* they make their money.

If you don't want to compromise your heart or your values to make money, then this book is for you. If you want to find success without sacrificing peace, you want to stop chasing clients and money, and you want to host effective, heart-centered calls, you've come to the right place.

While I'm going to share my sales method and philosophy with you, please understand that I'm not providing scripts. I won't tell you the exact words to use with prospective clients. I don't have any one-liners, and I don't have advice on tactics that involve manipulation or trickery. I will, however, teach you the following:

- How to ditch the script and trust your intuition.

- How to structure your coaching offers for maximum impact.

- Why single sessions don't work, and the importance of creating a partnership.

- How to tap into your feminine sales energy, and why it's good for all genders.

- How to set yourself up for success by creating boundaries.

- The behaviors that attract clients, and the behaviors that turn them off.

- How to present your coaching skills and all you have to offer without giving away coaching for free.

- How to make your sales transformational rather than transactional.

- How to receive for your work so you can give from abundance.

- How to host calls properly and enroll prospective clients into your program.

- How to talk about and accept money.

IT'S NOT ABOUT YOU

I can teach you everything I know, and you can implement all of it, but you won't be successful until you realize that coaching *is not about you*. When you make your offerings and services about you—your qualifications, confidence, or self-worth—you are taking a self-centered approach. You aren't putting the client first. The reality is your program allows you to create a client-coach partnership. This takes the onus off you, and you simply become the client's guide as they make their choices.

When coaches lack confidence or think their offerings are about them, they don't charge enough for their services. There's an issue of the heart that causes them to feel unworthy. Or they feel that a high price may be cheating the client when in fact, the high price *empowers* them to show up and take action.

If you're struggling to see your worth, then nothing I teach you in this book will matter. You have to address the heart issue and work through any issues you may have with charging and accepting money. The work begins with a shift to the mindset of abundance.

When I first began coaching and consulting, I honestly thought the police were going to come for me. I was getting paid to show up, and it felt too good to be true. I was earning money for my time, despite the fact that I wasn't producing any material output. How was it okay for me to accept money when nothing tangible had exchanged hands? It *had* to be illegal!

I realized I was uneasy about accepting money for coaching because in our society, we're accustomed to receiving for output. We receive by *doing*, not by showing up. This is where the mindset shift comes in. You have to get comfortable with accepting money for your gifts, talents, and all you have to offer. We'll discuss all of this in detail in Chapter 8.

A FRAMEWORK FOR THE CURIOUS BRAIN AND THE ANXIOUS BRAIN

We have a curious brain, and we have an anxious brain. In sales, we want to activate the curious brain and calm the anxious brain, and in order to do that, we have to give both of them what they want. And what do they want? They want a framework, something to guide them. A framework, unlike a script, helps us to stop focusing on our "performance," and helps us stay embodied instead. We can get curious about the prospective client in front of us.

When we give both of these brains what they want (or at least, what they *think* they want), then the anxious brain is calmed, and the curious brain can lean in and start doing the things we want it to do. However, this takes training.

In the pages that follow, we'll talk about sales methods that differ greatly from what you've been taught, and why they work. You'll begin to view sales through a different lens and have real conversations with clients. I'll provide you with the guide and nudge to get started, but the intent is to activate your curious brain.

I agree wholeheartedly with the founders of the Co-Active Coaching Model that "people are naturally creative, resourceful, and whole."[1] Everything you need to be successful is within both you and the client. And once you realize that, you can throw out your script and simply use an aligned sales call framework as your guide.

While I'm providing a guide for sales, I'll also provide access to additional resources along the way. There are PDFs and website links throughout the book that are exclusive to you, the reader, and I believe they will be a tremendous help to you.

---

1 "What Is Co-Active?" Co-Active® Training Institute, accessed September 8, 2022, https://coactive.com/about/what-is-coactive/.

My overall hope is that this book will inspire you. But even more so, I hope you'll learn from my experiences, because growth and success begin with learning.

Now, let's begin our journey into heart-centered sales!

TURN YOUR COACHING INTO A HIGH-TICKET OFFER

I sat in the therapist's office, looking at the Ivy League school degree on her wall. I had just finished spilling the details of my life to her: my ten-year marriage was on the rocks, my three young children were stressing me out, and I was burning the candle at both ends. I was spiraling out, and I longed for some real help.

Imagine my disappointment when, at the end of our sixty-minute session, she didn't propose a plan of action or provide me with next steps. All she said was, "I'd love to work with you. You can schedule another session with me whenever you're ready. Have a great day."

I left her office, got into my car, and sobbed. My mental state was no different than when I entered, and I felt helpless.

THE MISTAKE

What could this therapist have done differently? How could she have truly helped me? And how could *she* have benefited from helping me? I picture her saying something more like this:

"Michelle, you're ten years into your marriage. What you're experiencing is completely normal. I don't know that I can save your marriage, but if you commit to doing the work, you'll start to feel better. I can commit to helping you through this process.

"I propose we work together for three months. We'll meet every other week, and you'll have homework for the weeks we don't meet. Your homework will consist of going on a date with your spouse and hanging out with each child one-on-one. You'll also set aside personal time for yourself.

"So let's get you scheduled! I'll put you on the calendar, and I'll give you your first homework assignment."

This would have been an offer I couldn't refuse—I would have signed up right away. She could have named her price, and I would have paid it, hands down. Actually, I probably would have paid twice as much because I desperately needed the help.

Had the therapist made me this offer, she truly would have helped me. She would have created a partnership. She would have also eliminated her own stress in selling me single sessions, wondering if and when I would return, and wondering how I was doing in the meantime.

Most importantly, we would have seen results!

IT'S A PARTNERSHIP

If I had continued with this therapist, I can guess that all I would have done is word vomit in every session, doing nothing to create change in between. Based on our initial meeting, it appeared that she wasn't going to give me the tools and support I needed to make changes in my life. She would have listened to me, but the mere act of listening wouldn't have *helped* me. I didn't need a therapist; I needed a coach.

A coach would hold me accountable for my role in making progress. A coach would know that the magic happens *between* sessions, and that, in the course of our work together, we'd create a partnership.

So, what makes a good client-coach partnership? Three things:

- A specific start date

- A specific end date

- The exchange of money

When you enter into a partnership, there is a clear beginning. You choose a date in the near future to formally start. It also has a specific end date, typically three, six, or twelve months later. Lastly, funds are exchanged commensurate with the desired transformation and the support the coach will provide.

I first learned this way of offering coaching from Laura Wieck, founder of the BodyMind Coaching Certification Program. It's so simple, yet so profound, and it has changed the lives (and bank accounts) of thousands of coaches and clients around the world. As we go through the fundamentals of sales in the following chapters, I invite you to keep this "client-coach partnership" concept in mind.

To be clear, this process will create income and wealth for you. I'll never apologize for that truth. You should 100 percent celebrate making a whole pile of money, but that's not the primary goal of coaching. The primary goal is serving the client, and in order to do that well, a beginning, an end, and an exchange of money are not optional. This structure is essential to your success, and that of the client.

CREATING A PARTNERSHIP

Okay, so let me talk about this therapist one more time. What if, instead of treating me like a customer, she had wrapped me up in love? What if she'd comforted me with the core beliefs of coaching, and created a partnership? What if she had said something like this:

"I'm not here to fix you. You are whole and perfect just as you are. I'm here to be a guide for you—to help you find and take your next steps during this difficult time. Whatever you want to do or become, you can do or become in real life. And that means you won't need me forever."

Can you feel the difference between this interaction and the way she actually ended our session together?

If you care about how you feel every day and serving others, creating a client-coach partnership should get you excited! You'll empower your clients, and you'll be able to help them in exactly the way they want to be helped.

Learning to sell your coaching services isn't optional. It's vital to your success, and to that of your client. Your work matters. Set up the partnership early on and watch as you and the client both thrive.

NO MORE SINGLE SESSIONS

A client-coach partnership greatly benefits the client, and it also makes you, the coach, much happier, because you'll no longer sell single sessions. This might not seem like a big deal to you, but the fact is, single sessions *keep you stuck.*

And once you go down Single Sessions Street with a client, it's hard to turn around. I'll illustrate this point by telling you about Alison.

Alison used to sell single sessions for $75 each. To pay the bills, she had to sell a hundred sessions a month. It was heavy. It was hard. Every week she had to sell and resell, sell and resell.

Eventually, Alison decided to change her approach. She started selling three-month client-coach partnerships, where she'd work with her clients every other week. In between sessions, she sent a worksheet, meditation, podcast, and other tools to support the client. She charged $500 a month for three months, or a total of $1,500.

With single sessions, Alison might have made $75 every other week from one client. In three months, she would have made a little more than $450, assuming that she could get the same person to keep signing up. And there was even more of a downside: any support she gave a client outside of their scheduled session came out of her own pocket, since she was only charging for the session time itself. Essentially, she was coaching *for free,* and Alison didn't like the way that made her feel.

By switching to three-month client-coach partnerships, Alison was able to charge three times as much. More importantly, she could give her clients the type of ongoing support that would lead to real change. Clients want full support around their goal, and now Alison was able to provide hers with exactly that, while alleviating the pressure of scraping by to pay her bills. Even better, because clients paid more, they were more motivated to show up and do the work. Clients now viewed Alison's coaching as a valuable investment!

It's not Alison's fault that she used to sell single sessions. She, like so many other coaches, was taught how to facilitate coaching conversations, but was taught nothing about pricing, support, and how to structure a program. So she found herself on a treadmill, selling single sessions for $75.

Obviously, there's *a lot* of stress involved in selling single sessions. Offering client-coach partnerships relieves that stress and allows you to help clients even more by holding them accountable.

NUMBERS MATTER

I usually teach that $1,500 is a great place to start for a three-month partnership. There are several reasons for this, which we'll discuss throughout the book. But I also believe that you should never use someone else's price. Just make sure you're charging for *all* your time: the emails, the tools, the worksheets, and everything else you provide between sessions.

Don't be scared to charge thousands, even if you're a new coach. Keep in mind that you aren't charging for single sessions; you're charging for the entire client-coach partnership.

I promise that having three-, six-, or twelve-month client-coach partnerships at a set price will be worth it. Instead of having a hundred, small, $75 conversations, you have *one conversation* about money. This allows both of you to turn your attention to where it belongs: the coaching.

DRIVING ON AUTOPILOT

At this point, even though you know that it's necessary to offer client-coach partnerships, you will still feel uncomfortable the first time you do it. Stepping into anything new is uncomfortable. You're not quite sure what you're doing. You're feeling out the steps. But then you do it a second time, and it's a little easier. Each time after that is easier still, and soon it becomes second nature. Eventually, this previously uncomfortable thing becomes matter of fact, like water flowing through you.

This process is like learning to drive a car. I'm sure you were nervous the first time you drove. It required a conscious effort every time you moved your foot or turned the wheel. You had to remind yourself to turn on the blinker. But after driving for a long time, the process became automatic. Now, you think about which route to take and focus on the road, not the car. Now, you drive on autopilot.

As you step into running your business by offering client-coach partnerships, and as you practice this new, different kind of sales conversation, it will feel the same. No matter how awkward or uncomfortable it feels at first, it will get easier. You'll build muscle memory. You'll talk about money, lean in, speak up, and say what you think. You'll be able to serve clients without making it about you, and you can have natural, authentic, heart-centered sales conversations you feel good about. We'll dive into what this looks like in Chapter 8.

BECOMING YOUR MOST AUTHENTIC SALES SELF

Most coaches have only ever approached sales with a quantity or production mindset. If that's you, making this shift to heart-centered sales may sound difficult. You may be so used to the mantra of "sell, sell, sell" that anything else seems impossible. This is not your fault! There's no way you could have known about heart-centered sales before unless someone taught you.

In the following pages, I want to show you what I've learned from personally hosting over four hundred sales calls, enrolling hundreds of clients into the BodyMind ($15,000+) Coaching Program, and leading their million-dollar sales team.

A large shift in mindset and a tiny shift in how you offer and structure your services will set you up for an incredibly rewarding, fulfilling, abundant career.

Remember, your work as a coach doesn't just impact the clients you serve. It trickles into the everyday lives of their spouses, kids, co-workers, and families. We've all experienced this ourselves as coaches—the impact of this work is life-changing and affects generations. Your life's work is not possible without heart-centered sales. You can do this!

To start, you need to think about who you want to be as a salesperson. How do you want to show up? How can you be your best and most authentic self? What would that look like in practice?

In the next chapter, we'll explore the differences between masculine and feminine sales styles, and how the feminine style supports you and the prospective client when it comes to selling coaching. (Yes, the feminine style works better for men in this case, too). We'll discover your natural tendencies, take stock of where you are, and continue on the journey of getting you where you want to be.

THE FEMININE WAY OF SALES

YEARS AGO, I WAS LUCKY ENOUGH TO HAVE A FANTASTIC coach who helped me transform my approach to sales. After our calls together, I felt like anything was possible, and I always sold a program after I talked with her. But during one of our many sessions together, she looked up at me, and there was a long pause before she spoke again.

"Michelle," she said, "you have a very masculine sales energy."

My heart started beating wildly, and I got hot all over. What did she mean by "masculine sales energy"? I was pretty sure that everyone I knew would have described me as a feminine woman. I felt around my upper lip for a hint of a mustache. Nothing. How could I possibly have masculine sales energy?

With a small voice, I asked her to explain.

She continued, "Michelle, you're naturally leaning into masculine sales tactics. You follow up with the client multiple times. You make yourself available without setting boundaries, and you try to prove the value of your offer by listing all the 'stuff.'" She went on and on, explaining that I gave away my coaching for free, I discounted, and I hosted long sales calls. I chased the sale—any sale—and I wanted to win no matter the cost.

I took in her words, and I realized I wasn't really selling. I was acting like I had something to prove.

All of these tactics had come from the sales playbook I had been given. I blindly followed it, never considering that there could be another way—these were the only "rules" of sales I had ever known, and I had started to pass them on to our new sales team as we enrolled clients into a high-priced coaching program. Follow up, follow up, follow up. Make seven calls to get one yes. These methods had worked for me in the past, so why would I change things up?

Because women don't want to work that way. Really, it doesn't matter what gender you identify with. Deep down, **no one** wants to work this way.

I was starting to see that there was, in fact, another way. Could it be possible? Could I be 100 percent in alignment with my values, boundaries, and energy, and still get a yes? Could I stop chasing and still catch? I was intrigued.

HOW DID I WANT TO *FEEL*?

I'm what you might call a "feeler." A more familiar term is *empath*. I feel and care deeply, sometimes to my detriment. A single sales call could take up my mental space for an entire day. I'd lie awake at night wondering how I could turn a maybe into a yes.

As the mom of three boys and two fur babies, I only had four hours a day to work when I first started selling coaching. And I had even less mental energy to spare. Sales calls were draining much of my mental space because I was out of integrity, and I knew something had to change.

This way of working wasn't sustainable for me. I knew that what I was selling could change lives, families, even generations. I needed to find a way to serve clients—the right clients—and successfully enroll them, while not letting my values fall away.

I always ask clients to envision how they want to feel when they achieve their goal, and then work backward from there. Now, it was time for me to do this for myself. So I sat back and began to work from my heart center. How did feminine sales energy look and feel?

For me, feminine sales was about receiving, rather than chasing. I asked myself what I wanted to receive from each interaction, and how I wanted to *feel* at the end of every sales call.

Here's what came out: I want to feel connected, relaxed, of service, 100 percent my authentic self, with no BS, and no playing small. I wanted to be seen and truly see the prospective client on the other end of the video call. I desired the same warm, fuzzy feelings for them, too. I wanted them to feel embodied, relaxed, seen, and heard. And of course, understood like never before.

So how could all of this be achieved? What system needed to be in place to support myself, my clients, and the feelings I desired for all of us?

I got to work and figured it out.

A FEW CALLS PER MONTH IS ALL YOU NEED

Traditional sales methods are typically masculine, and they can be effective in the right situations, but they work for two reasons: a company has a mammoth advertising budget, and they have salespeople with dedicated time. I'm talking about the kind of time you'd need to spend calling twenty-one people to get three yeses. If you're reading this book, odds are you have neither.

And you don't need them.

Consider this. Instead of taking sales calls all day long, what if you only spoke with prospective clients who would be a good fit? What if you could enroll one out of two, or even *every* person you spoke with?

With just a handful of calls every month, you would thrive!

Don't get me wrong. This is not about having a better client come through the door—this approach relies on your ability to connect. You can go a mile wide and an inch deep, spending your energy chasing everyone and following up, or you can work smarter. By showing up as your 100 percent embodied self, by making people feel *seen and heard*, you'll project a richer experience. You'll attract (and enroll) more of the right clients.

You can *receive*.

MASCULINE VS. FEMININE SALES ENERGY

To effectively sell coaching, it's important for you to understand the differences between masculine and feminine sales energy. Having an awareness of the two types of energy will help you decide how you want to show up for sales calls, rather than showing up based on what you've been taught, or what society has conditioned you to believe. Understanding the two energies empowers you to choose the one that will best serve you and the prospective client.

The typical masculine sales energy is unmistakable—it's aggressive. Male energy is challenging and goes out to get the sale, like it's a hunt. It's a "chasing" energy, which means it wants to prove the value of the sale. This can result in the use of scare tactics or badgering the client. The details of the task are less important than getting the task done.

The typical feminine sales energy is different—the client's needs matter as much as the coach's. Not more than, but equal to. When you're in this type of energy, if you sell something that isn't best for the client, you consider it a bad day.

Masculine sales energy is available at any time. It does whatever it takes to get the sale and adjusts everything else in life to make it happen. Feminine sales energy is less available and spends more time preparing. It sets the stage for the client to have a full, embodied experience. Feminine energy connects, invites, and creates space for both the client and coach to receive.

A colleague with a masculine sales energy would ask me if I'm a high-ticket closer. A colleague with a more feminine approach, on the other hand, would ask me, "Are you speaking to aligned clients? How are your client relationships?" Notice the difference?

Masculine sales energy has value and can bring a lot to the table. It shows up boldly, has confidence, and doesn't take anything personally. This energy works well for professional salespeople whose sole job is to sell a tangible product.

However, if you're selling coaching, you enter a sales conversation with a feminine energy and a different goal in mind. You're there to figure out if you're aligned with the person you're speaking to and vice versa.

While the feminine energy has the client's needs in mind, it's also important to be bold and brave (typically more masculine) when sharing your coaching services. To be most effective in sales and coaching, you want to create your own blend of the masculine and feminine styles.

CAN I HELP?

When I'm on a call with a prospective client, I align with my feminine sales energy and listen to truly understand. This is all with the intent of helping them uncover their true problem, and to see if we're aligned to work together. When I listen to a client, I consider the following:

- Do our personalities fit?

- Can I help this person?

- Do I want to help them?

- Are they coachable?

- Am I aligned with their needs?

- What choice do they need to make?

- How can I hold space to support them in that choice?

As a coach, I care deeply. I want the client to be successful, and I want us to enjoy our shared experience. So I take a feminine approach with open conversation and engaged listening to discover the answers to these questions, because listening and true understanding are at the heart of feminine sales energy.

THE COST OF THE OLD WAY

Change is hard. Even good change feels uncomfortable. However, exploring our previous style of selling can help us determine what we want to keep and what we want to toss.

Let's imagine you continue to approach sales calls with the traditional, unwritten rules of sales, which we've established are typically more masculine. What would that look like?

- You allow the client to book a call at a time when you may not be fully present.

- You defer to them, as if they are always right.

- You discount the price of your services to make the sale.

- You answer objections, as if any objection can be overcome with the right words.

- You try to convince with logic, as if people make decisions based on logic. (A few do, but not many. More on this later!)

- You use scare tactics.

- You chase, with many aggressive follow ups.

- You say what you have to say to close the sale at any cost.

If you exclusively follow the traditional rules of sales when selling coaching, you set yourself up for failure. Not only that, but it may also end up costing you a great deal. But how? Why?

To give an example, if you use scare tactics to sell, it means that a client is enrolling in your program *because they're scared,* not because they're inspired or aligned. Fear will make them a difficult client, and this will backfire on both of you.

In fact, a misaligned client could cost you *thousands and thousands of dollars.* I don't mean that you'll see money being drained from your bank account immediately, but you will lose money in the end, and much more. Here's what I mean:

First, you'll lose energy because the client doesn't follow through. Since their participation in your program is fear-based, they aren't truly motivated, and it won't be sustainable.

Second, a misaligned client won't get great results, and you'll begin to question your value as a coach. It won't feel good to show up every day. You want your coaching conversations to be fully aligned with your values, and since these conversations won't be, the relationship won't be sustainable for either you or the client.

And third, the energy expended for this client will actually block you from bringing in new clients. You'll be so focused on this troublesome client that you'll begin to question yourself and your abilities. You'll show up on social media differently. The doubt will show up in the tone of your emails, or in your energy on your next sales call. You could tell a potential client that everyone you're working with is having the most amazing experience, but if the energy isn't there, they'll feel and sense that you aren't being honest.

So the old way of selling can lead to a misaligned client-coach partnership, costing you way too much. This leads to lost opportunities with other clients. You lose time and waste resources. And if the client is unhappy, it can lead to bad reviews and affect your reputation.

I know, that was a lot to take in. But using traditional sales tactics really will cost you!

THE ENERGY SHIFT

Moving into feminine sales energy means changing how you think about sales. For example, I no longer "sell." I am not a high-ticket closer—I offer client-coach partnerships for large dollar amounts. I am an embodied leader who helps people make empowered choices, and these choices will better their lives forever.

This shift in how I think and speak means that I am secure in myself. I don't have to "close a sale," because I am confident there will be another client knocking on my door after this one. I'm free to be soft and gentle. I can exude stereotypical feminine energy. I can choose to serve the person in that moment, regardless of the outcome.

When that coach looked me in the eyes and told me I had masculine sales energy, I felt like she had slapped me across the face. My immediate reaction was disbelief, but then I opened my heart and mind to the concept of masculine and feminine sales energies, and something inside shifted.

I tried changing the way I conducted sales calls. I began preparing for embodied calls, allowing myself to be fully present. I did not call the client directly. Instead, I approached the call with a new mindset: we were meeting together on the line face-to-face. I allowed myself to receive. Sure enough, the floodgates opened. The things people started to tell me!

It felt *right*. I served the clients, gracefully allowing them to say "no" and move on, or to be empowered to make a huge investment in themselves without fear. I held space. I honored the importance of their choice in that moment.

And it worked. More clients enrolled in a shorter period of time, at a higher price. Plus, I felt better. I was no longer lying awake at night. I began making a great living, without all the stress. And you know what else? Client results skyrocketed, too! They were committed, they trusted me, and most importantly, they trusted in themselves.

At times, traditional sales can feel heavy and hard, but feminine sales always feels empowering. It allows you to host sales calls that both you and your client will fondly remember for the rest of your lives. It empowers the client, and it also sets you up for living and working in a fully embodied way that fits your values. It brings in a good income, and potentially incredible wealth.

Tapping Into Your Feminine Sales Energy Before a Call

How do you shift your mindset prior to your sales calls? How do you allow yourself to be present, connected, and fully tapped into your feminine sales energy? You get embodied.

By this I mean you calm your anxious mind, slow down your breathing, and get inwardly connected. An embodiment practice such as yoga, breathwork, a walk, or a happy dance to your favorite tune will all work. Your job is to find what works for you! Experiment until you find a method that best supports you and know that this practice can change and evolve over time.

In addition to a physical practice, your office space can support a calm mind and body, too. By adding your favorite crystal, flowers, candle, or picture to your space, you'll have physical reminders prompting you to stay calm and internally connected throughout the entire call.

Lastly, be sure you won't be interrupted. Put a sign on the door letting others know not to come in and silence your phone. By doing these things you tap into your feminine sales energy and set both you and your client up for a life-changing sales call!

WRITING YOUR (SALES) LOVE STORY

As a mom, being present with my kids is critical. If I took the traditional approach to sales and constantly chased and followed up, it would take energy away from them. I'd have to be available to clients and prospects all the time, making it difficult to be in the right headspace with my family.

Well, my son recently confirmed that I'm in the right headspace. We were driving home from swim practice, and out of nowhere, he said, "Mom, it's weird how much you like your job." He's ten! I think he caught me smiling in the car, which is not unusual.

Smiles often come out of nowhere when I think about a conversation I had with a client. I thought about this for a while, and I realized that people who are in love will smile out of nowhere. This could only mean that *I'm in love with my job*!

Feminine sales is all about falling in love with the process, and with all of the steps that bring your services to others. And guess what? *You* get to create this process! This is your love story to write.

What will your relationship look like? That's up to you because you get to paint the picture. You get to create something that makes you smile while you drive your minivan home from swim practice.

HAPPY AND FREE

Leaning into the feminine way of selling allows you to receive rather than strive. Tuning into this energy unlocks richness in your life and work. When you tap into your feminine sales energy, you will become unstoppable.

Approaching sales in this way creates so much freedom. You'll be happier. You'll enter a place where results can happen naturally, without all the worrying and chasing. This way of working will feel amazing, open up new worlds, and people will be naturally attracted to you.

Now that you know how the feminine style of selling allows you to receive, let's move on to helping you set the stage for successful sales calls before you even say that first "hello." What I'm going to share with you in this next chapter is simple, yet so powerful. It came about after taking hundreds of sales calls, and making shift after shift to empower the client, and myself as an enrollment coach and sales team manager. Do not skip the next chapter!

SETTING YOURSELF UP FOR SUCCESS

I WAS TEN YEARS OLD. MY HAIR WAS WET. I WAS WEARING a parka over my swimsuit, and it was cold. I was sitting outside of the YMCA in Southern California, in the dark, waiting for my mom to come pick me up.

The scenario always played out the same way. After swim practice, other parents would see me waiting and they'd ask if I needed a ride. Sometimes a parent would awkwardly wait with me.

I'd use quarters to call my mom from the pay phone.

"I'm almost there, I'm almost there," she'd always tell me. But she never was.

It happened time and time again. "Mom, where the heck are you?"

"I'm almost there."

I'd never felt so lonely in my life as I did those times when I sat in the dark, day after day, sopping wet and waiting. My mom wasn't coming to pick me up. I felt like she didn't care about me, like she didn't value me at all.

I made a vow at age ten that, come hell or high water, I would never leave my child alone like that. I would be the lady mowing people down to get to my child on time.

Decades later, as an adult with a coaching business, my sales calls sometimes ran long. Then one afternoon, I pulled up to the carpool line of my son's Montessori school and saw him standing alone on the street corner, hand in hand with the teacher. My heart sank. He was the last one to be picked up. I was doing the same thing to him that my mom did to me.

I knew in my heart that no sale was more important than this tiny human being waiting for his momma. I buckled him in, kissed him all over his beautiful face, and vowed to never be late again.

In order to keep that vow, something had to change.

THE SHORTER WAY TO SUCCESS

I had just scheduled my first forty-five-minute sales call, and I was determined to keep it at forty-five minutes. I set multiple timers. I was not going to fail my children the way my mom had failed me. But the call ran over.

So I tried again and again. I paid attention to what worked, and what didn't work. I learned that if I didn't prepare carefully, the call would run over. If I fell into coaching a prospective client on the sales call, it would run over. Because I had so little time, I was forced to learn habits that would eventually create my success.

You see, one of the fastest ways to lose a sale is to coach someone during a sales call. You've probably done it, as it's very common. You get on a call with the goal of having a sales conversation, and you give coaching away for free instead. The person has not agreed to it or made an investment in it, and they inevitably get off topic. The coaching does not land well.

Even worse, by letting the person get off topic, you lose command of the call. You don't demonstrate the type of coach that you'll be. You lose the energy, and you lose the sale.

It was a happy accident that my forty-five-minute time limit forced me to stop coaching on these calls. Suddenly, I was enrolling more clients.

But what was I doing differently, exactly? What had changed?

I had been hosting long calls, thinking I was being "nice." I wanted to be kind, so I let the client wander off into a story. But no one wants to pay thousands of dollars to hire a coach that isn't able to reel them in. I lost command of the calls, and I lost the opportunities, over and over again.

When I forced myself to limit calls to forty-five minutes, I was forced to take charge. I was forced to have confidence. I allowed myself to say, "Hey, I'm going to interrupt you. Let's bring you back." The time limit was a forcing mechanism for authority. On top of that, it forced me to be prepared.

SETTING BOUNDARIES

One afternoon, I found myself, as many coaches do, messaging with someone online who needed sales support. I had met Eric through an online course that taught coaches how to write better emails. He'd asked if I could support him in improving his sales skills. I told him I could, and suggested we have a call to see if we were a fit.

He responded quickly. "I'm available on Sunday, so try me then." I read and reread the words in the message.

The gremlin on one shoulder said, "Leave it alone and just call him on Sunday."

The feminine goddess on my other shoulder reminded me of what I knew very well to be true: calling a client directly is a chasing energy. He'd likely be doing yard work when I tried to call him. Or he wouldn't be able to pick up. Or he'd be multi-tasking in some way and not fully focused on our call.

So, I put on my big girl pants and messaged him back. "Hey, I don't work on the weekends, and my schedule is a little nutty next week. I hope one of these times works for you. I'm really looking forward to connecting." Then I dropped him my scheduling link and waited with bated breath (dramatic, I know, but 100 percent true).

A few minutes later: *ding*! He had filled out my pre-call questionnaire and scheduled a call. I released a deep exhale, smiled, and ran full speed ahead to pick up my kiddos from school.

BOUNDARIES ARE NOT OPTIONAL

For a prospective client to feel and receive support during sales calls, a structure needs to exist. It lays the foundation for the relationship going forward and holds the client and myself to a higher standard. Setting boundaries around when you host calls, the length of the calls, and the format (face-to-face vs. phone) are all vital to the outcome. I learned this only after hosting hundreds of calls.

In the beginning, I felt selfish for insisting on a hard forty-five-minute call time. But I found out that boundaries aren't selfish or dramatic in any way. They allow the client to make space for themselves, to show up for a call fully prepared, and to value their time. Boundaries encourage people to respect *themselves*. Being "nice" (which usually equates to being too accommodating) may feel good in the moment, but it's an active disservice to your client.

Think about it. Would you respect a lawyer who let you walk all over them? No. But if they held you to a specific time frame, you'd show up five minutes early, with all your homework done.

That respect for time starts immediately on a sales call. The setup of that call is just as important as any of the words you are going to say on the actual call. I'll explain what I mean by the setup, or structure, in a moment.

Setup isn't sexy; it's not a one-liner or a zinger you can insert at the beginning or end of your call that will get the client to say yes. (Which, by the way, only works in movies, and maybe for "bro marketers" on a very good day). Heart-centered coaches and service providers live in a different world.

These small shifts in your setup will yield massive results. As you learn and grow, you will analyze, customize, and modify your own setup over time. But the key takeaway here is that *boundaries are not optional.*

SALES CALL SETUP

When you set up a sales call the right way, you demonstrate what the coaching relationship is going to be like, how the client should treat you, and how they should treat themselves. Setting up the call the right way allows both coach and client to show up to the call embodied, fiercely focused, and ready to connect. Keep reading to learn the Five Golden Rules of Sales Call Setup. These will help you host productive, successful sales calls, and set you up for a yes before you even say "hello."

The Five Golden Rules of Sales Call Setup

1. Host calls face-to-face.

Want to increase trust and decrease the time it takes for a prospective client to decide to hire you? Then host a call face-to-face! I'm being serious. When you can see the other person's body language, either in person or on video, you gain important insight into their thoughts and feelings, *and they can do the same with you.* So many vital cues—a sigh, an eye roll, or a distraction—are missed if you're only connecting via audio.

Guess what else? Your clients will show up to the call well-dressed, hair brushed, fully prepared, and sitting down. Consider how different a start to the relationship this is versus you dialing the client on a Sunday and trying to "catch" them. Not to mention we've all had that client who's shopping at Target during the call. It's maddening! There's no way *anyone* can connect with you, feel into their desired outcome, understand their actual problem, and envision what's possible while they're browsing the vitamin aisle at Target.

The Gentle Release

You will never enroll a multitasking client. Trust me. If a prospective client is multitasking, *end the call.* You should also end the call if warning bells are going off in your mind about the client, or when you can sense they aren't going to be a good fit. You can do this kindly with a phrase my colleagues have coined, the "gentle release."

With a gentle release, you tell the client you feel that the program isn't the right next step for them. Then you suggest another action item, such as watching a free training video of yours, or asking them to do more research. This allows you to end the call by being truthful and authentic, and it's respectful of the client's time, energy, and feelings, as well as your own.

I've worked with hundreds of amazing heart-centered coaches who have a million excuses for why they don't want to host calls face-to-face. Reasons like: I just don't want to get dressed, my background isn't great, I don't want to bother the client, or I'm old school, and so are my clients. My absolute favorite? *The phone works just fine for me!* Well, that might be true, but face-to-face will work better. So unless you're enrolling 100 percent of the prospective clients you speak with, turn on your computer camera and settle in. No more excuses!

One last point before we move on. Remember, we're leaning into the feminine energy of receiving. When we dial the client, we are "chasing," and we head into the masculine energy of sales. Instead, we relax and meet in the middle on neutral territory, in a videoconference room.

This way, you and the client are both set up for success before you even say "hello."

2. Only take calls at times that work for you.

I take sales and coaching calls at 9:00 and 11:00 a.m., Monday through Friday. These are the times when I am at my best. I'm fed, settled, and the house is quiet. This block of time also gives me space to do my embodiment work before my calls, allowing me to be 100 percent present (more on this later). These two times also never get in the way of my kids' soccer practice, swim practice, music lessons, and so on. And since I work out early in the mornings, the call times don't mess with that, either. These times are ideal, and I show up ready to serve and connect with my full self.

What times work best for you? Even if you don't have clients yet, you have kids, dogs, workouts, and meals to prepare. You have a life, and your work should support that—it shouldn't be the other way around. Taking calls when you're at your best will lead to more sales and a happier, healthier *you*.

3. Don't allow prospective clients to reschedule.

Wait, what? Yup. I mean it. Your time is valuable, and if you don't respect it, your clients won't either.

You see, the boundaries you demonstrate during sales calls have to align with the values you're going to teach during your coaching programs. If you allow prospective clients to reschedule missed calls, you're not holding them accountable to their commitments; you're not demonstrating what it's like to value your time, and theirs. You don't exhibit the values of a million-dollar coach by allowing them to reschedule calls.

To be a great coach, you must:

- hold fierce boundaries

- honor both you and your client's time

- hold clients accountable to their commitments

So, be a great coach before you even say "hello." Don't allow prospective clients who no-show on a sales call to reschedule.

Ever. Some of you may be naysayers of this rule. Maybe you've enrolled someone after allowing them to reschedule. Know this: they were the exception, not the rule. I'd also be willing to bet that this same client rescheduled more than once during your time together, costing you time and money, and making it difficult to hold them to their commitments.

How do I kindly let prospective clients know that I value their time and mine, and that I do not reschedule? What does this boundary look like in practice? It's too detailed to share here, but it's included in a resource that's available for you at the end of this chapter. This resource will also help you to fully implement everything you're learning here.

4. Limit calls to forty-five minutes.

Remember the story I told at the beginning of this chapter? The one with ten-year-old me, cold and wet, wearing a parka over my swimsuit, always waiting for my mom to pick me up from swim practice? The one where I vowed to never be late picking up my own kids, only to have my son be the last one picked up from school because I let a sales call run too long?

As my heart broke over failing to keep this promise, I realized I needed better setup, systems, and structure. Since I could only work four hours a day when my kids were young, I had to work smarter. I knew I wanted to take at least two calls per day, and with breaks and other work, that meant I could do two forty-five-minute calls.

When I made the change to the length of my calls, I let clients know at the top of each call that I had forty-five minutes to connect, and I confirmed that this was okay with them before we started. It always was.

What happened next blew my mind! The yeses began rolling in with ease. In retrospect, the reason was obvious. I was demonstrating what it would be like to work with me. I honored my time, and the client's time, through structure and boundaries. I stayed in command of the call and followed a proven structure for the flow of the call itself.

Don't Give It Away for Free

Coaches are naturally kind, caring, considerate people who want to fix a prospective client's problem. For this reason, you may have a tendency to allow a client to go into "story" during a sales call because you want to serve but doing this can backfire. And if you dive in and start giving specific advice, you're likely to lose the sale.

I'm not saying you shouldn't share how you work with clients or give examples of successes you've had. I'm saying you should steer clear of getting into the nitty-gritty of coaching. This type of in-depth coaching is reserved for paying clients and, although counterintuitive, a client is less likely to make the choice to work with you if you get into problem-solving mode during a sales call.

Trying to appeal to the client's logical brain by coaching them around their problem doesn't work, because it takes their attention and focus away from their desired transformation. Instead, they place their focus on the action or work they need to do, and they'll subconsciously list all the reasons why they can't do it. Coaching on specifics during a sales call puts you right back at square one with an overwhelmed client who is unsure of their next steps.

Keeping it high-level and focusing on the big picture is the best way to support the client. Don't overwhelm your client by giving away coaching for free! Instead, follow the Five Golden Rules to indirectly show off your coaching skills. You'll demonstrate fierce boundaries and your ability to keep a client on task and forward focused. You'll highlight your confidence, command, and expert status, while increasing the likelihood of a *yes*!

5. Don't allow prospective clients to schedule more than three days in advance.

I insist you limit your availability, my dear heart-centered coaches and service providers. Don't leave your calendar wide open. This is not just for your success, but for the sake of your heart. You know how I only take calls two times a day? I also only allow prospective clients to schedule three to four days in advance. As humans, we can get distracted very easily, and after a few days, we move on to the next thing. You will have no-shows if you let clients schedule calls any more than three (a maximum of four) days in advance—guaranteed.

This isn't personal. It's just true.

When you show your entire month as available, you convey the message that you're not busy, not in demand, and available anytime.

Remember Eric? He found a way to get on my calendar because it was important to him. He truly wanted to learn how to have the sales conversation and see his business thrive. If he was never able to speak at the times when I hosted calls, it wouldn't have worked out for us anyway. Being less available saved both of us the time and angst of trying to figure it out.

I hope this is starting to click for you. The Five Golden Rules I've just shared are simple ways in which you can step into your million-dollar coaching role with ease. Set boundaries! Demonstrate the badass and brilliant coach you are through your actions! It will set you and your clients up for success.

I invite you to resist the urge to explain or justify these golden rules to clients or to yourself. Don't apologize. Don't justify. Don't wait to sell until it feels perfect, and don't think you have to give away your services until you get your PhD. Start where you are, *because where you are is good enough*.

We have more sales fun to dive into. In the next chapter, we'll talk about what *should* be the goal of your sales calls.

To help you implement what you've learned in this chapter, I've created a printable PDF guide for the Five Golden Rules. To access this guide, visit www.michellerockwood.com/joyful.

THE GOAL IS NOT A YES

COACHES OFTEN THINK THEY CAN OBTAIN NEW CLIENTS through fancy marketing and razzle-dazzle sales tactics. I like marketing, and you know my background is in sales, but that basic assumption just isn't true. The way to enroll new clients who are aligned with your heart, business, and goals is to host an excellent sales call. A script won't be enough to accomplish this; instead, you need a framework. Remember, you aren't selling widgets. You're selling three-, six-, or twelve-month client-coach partnerships. And scripts aren't heart-centered—they lack the connection and depth needed to build the trust, rapport, and command needed to sell high-ticket coaching.

A specific framework such as my Five Steps to Choice, that I teach in my course called Unscripted Sales™, will allow you to show off your coaching skills *without giving away coaching for free*. It will highlight and feature your skills, abilities, and all you have to offer, giving the prospective client a taste of what it's like to work with you. This framework displays your ability to effectively lead and guide the client. It shows your confidence and ability to support them, and it will guide them to their next best choice.

The Five Steps to Choice came about years ago when I was a staff coach for the BodyMind Coaching Program. I had observed and worked with coaches in training for years, and the program founder kept saying over and over again, "Your job is to help your clients make a choice."

At my fifth in-person live training event for the program, it finally clicked. That's it! I realized our coach trainees needed a framework to do just that: to bring the client to a choice and help them make a decision around their next best steps. This was the element that was missing—coaches were skipping this vital step and jumping ahead to "pitch" their coaching.

This situation is not unique. I often find myself on the receiving end of such sales calls, where the salesperson fails to help me understand my actual problem and make a true choice as to my next step. Instead, they jump right into their pitch and fail to support me around the decision or choice I actually need to make.

If you're wondering why you weren't introduced to these concepts earlier in your certification program, it's because most coaching programs can't offer everything. They can't be a certification and sales course rolled into one. That'd be tough to pull off! You didn't learn about sales in your certification program because there just wasn't enough time to teach it.

Conducting an effective sales conversation is a critical skill to your coaching career, and if this concept is new to you, please don't be overwhelmed. In this chapter, I'll provide you with the elements of how to run an embodied sales call. I'll introduce you to the tools that will improve your calls immediately.

THE CHOICE CLIENTS WILL MAKE

If you're a coach with a lot to offer, of course you want people to enroll in your program. But enrollment can't be the primary goal of your sales calls. You can't approach calls with the mindset that you must enroll the client at all costs. Of course, I want yeses, and I want a lot of them, but I've learned that I can't get on my calls with the goal of obtaining a yes. It changes my energy.

If you approach a call with the mindset of selling to a prospective client right away, you won't ask the right questions. You'll exude a chasing, manipulative, masculine energy. If you dive in and talk about yourself, what you do, how you do it, and immediately talk about price, you'll put a damper on your success. If you exude a chasing energy, you might as well hang up, because you're wasting your time as well as the client's. Coming to a call with the sole intent of making the sale isn't good for anyone. It isn't heart-centered.

What if, instead, you came to the call with curiosity, inquiry, and a genuine desire to serve, projecting an amazing feminine sales energy? In this state, you are open to connecting and receiving. You set the stage for the client to have a thoughtful and transformative experience that day.

Here's the truth: the most important choice the client will make on a sales call has nothing to do with you. Yes, they will choose whether or not to work with you, but that's not the point. The choice they make will be focused on the particular problem that you will thoughtfully uncover together. Do they want to solve that problem and move forward right now? Are they committed to the change? If the answer is yes, working with you will become the clear and obvious next step. In the meantime, it's your job to hold space for their choice.

CURIOSITY IN ACTION

Let's say you're a health coach. A prospective client, Jim, comes into the sales call saying he wants to lose weight. He wants to understand *how* to lose weight and wants support while doing the work. But, for whatever reason, you feel desperate that day, and you're ready to sell to Jim at all costs.

You ask Jim a few questions. Simple ones, like how much weight he wants to lose, but the whole time you're thinking about the "how to" in your head. You start listing all the ways you can help. You explain why you're the best. You walk him through your weight loss program and explain what it can do for him. Then you give Jim a price.

Jim says he'll think about it, but he never gets back to you. Maybe you chase, and maybe you don't.

Now, what if, instead, you came to the call with a feminine energy? What if you approached every interaction with the intention of uncovering the problem Jim needs help with, and held space for him to choose his best path?

"What is it about losing weight that's most important to you?" you'll ask Jim.

He explains that he wants to run a marathon with his grandkids. Amazing!

"Tell me about the grandkids. Why is this connection so special?"

Jim stops and thinks, and then he starts to share his true problem. He wants to spend time with his grandkids and keep up with their interests. By listing all the ways you could help him lose weight, you completely miss Jim's true intentions and desires. He doesn't care that much about weight loss. He certainly isn't going to spend thousands of dollars to receive support for a goal that doesn't really matter. But when you got to the heart of his true choice, wow! Jim is ready.

A good sales conversation doesn't focus on the yes. It focuses on finding the true transformation the client wants and needs and opening the door to work together on that transformation. If you had sold him on something as surface as weight loss, Jim would have moved along without you. But when you sell him the connection with his grandkids, he sees the value of what you have to offer.

UNDERSTAND AND SERVE

In coaching circles, it's common to hear the cliché, "sell the transformation." This means that when you find the true choice the person wants to make, you can help them. On the call, you can explain how your work bridges the gap between where they are now and where they want to be. You can sell transformation and life-affirming connections with grandkids. If you don't understand what the client truly wants, you can't bridge that gap. You're just selling them weight loss steps.

Here's the critical idea: even if you were successful in getting the sale, Jim would never be fully happy with the surface weight loss steps. Somewhere down the line he would become a misaligned client, and as we talked about, that would cost you dearly and lead to stress upon stress.

Approach your calls with a genuine intention to understand. Help the client find the decision they need to make. Release the outcome of that decision by truly wanting what is best for them in that moment, whether they work with you or not. Have an attitude of service, and that attitude will set you free.

This attitude and approach will lead to more sales, and your program will be better for both you and the client. It will remove the chasing, masculine energy that poisons sales interactions from the start. And best of all, it will allow you to remove the BS and serve from a place of incredible feminine strength.

If you don't have the genuine intention to serve, you're selling the wrong product, or you're in the wrong field. People are much more attracted to you when you're willing to let go of the outcomes.

BE WILLING TO SAY NO

Sales conversations are like dating. Feeling like you can only carefully present your best front on a first date will always make you nervous, and it will make the other person wary. However, if you show up fully present and curious about whether or not this is a good fit for both of you, suddenly you are free. You are willing to end it after a cup of coffee, and you know it will be fine. You already have everything you need, so you don't need anyone else, but you are open to seeing what's possible.

Contrast that energy with someone who is desperate, coming to every date with an attitude and energy that screams, "I don't want to die alone!" How does that look and feel? That type of grasping isn't attractive, and it doesn't feel good to be on the receiving end of it. The best option is to show up to a sales conversation with confidence and curiosity, because this will feel good to you and to the client.

But just like a dating relationship, a coaching relationship should be wanted from both sides. It's not a decision the client makes on their own, and it's not a decision you make as a coach.

When you show up to every sales conversation with a curiosity and a willingness to let the client go, that attitude will seamlessly flow into the two of you working together if you make an aligned decision to do so.

Rather than trying to get a yes at all costs, come to the sales call with an open mind and with a willingness to say no. You will be happiest and most empowered when you feel you are able to make this choice. You get to decide if you can help and if you want to work with this person.

Ask yourself if this client aligned with you. Are there any red flags? Are they coachable? If you're going to spend a lot of intimate time with this person, it's in your financial (and emotional) best interest to make sure you feel as amazing about them as they do about you.

I've hosted hundreds of sales calls and enrolled client after client into amazing coaching programs. But I've also said no to taking people's money and enrolling them many times, knowing they were not a good fit for the program or that they would drain energy from paying clients. When I say no, I'm actually saying yes. I'm saying yes to more aligned clients. I'm saying yes to a better experience during the program, both for myself and for others. I'm saying yes to a higher likelihood of helping someone reach their full potential.

Let me make this clear once again: difficult clients don't get better. They'll be difficult straight through the program. They'll eat up far more time than any other client, they won't finish, or they won't reach a place of success. As I stated before, those issues will cost you.

Trust me. I've led a million-dollar sales team, managed multiple six-figure launches, and coached hundreds of coaches. You can learn from my mistakes. A misaligned client is a tremendous monetary and energetic drain. They will hurt your success rate and occupy entirely too much space in your mind. Taking them on is not worth it.

YOU CAN DO THIS

As coaches, our job is to help people make really big, really tough life decisions. We might support someone in making the decision to leave their marriage, stay in a job, have children, or other huge, life-altering choices. The stakes are high. So when you're able to help a client take their first step toward making an important choice in one forty-five-minute call, you give them a glimpse into what it will be like to work with you. You demonstrate the value of your coaching, and they're blown away.

When you approach the sales call with curiosity, you show the client that you can ask thoughtful questions, and you can help them find what is truly driving them. You show them you can guide them to their next best steps. You also show them that you'll do so in a way that will help them navigate their most important transformations, with their best interests in mind.

How beautiful is that? You can help someone without giving away coaching, while still showing off your coaching skills!

In the next chapters, we'll break down what this process looks like in action. What words should you use? How does one help a client come to a choice, specifically?

Intentions are great, but a framework is better.

Time for us to get specific.

HOW TO STOP THE SALES YUCK

I HAVE AN AMAZING FRIEND, ANNA, WHO CAN BUILD rapport with *anyone* in a matter of seconds. She quickly and effortlessly creates a deep, visceral, energetic connection with others. She can be at a gas station filling up her car or at a coffee house ordering a latte, and she'll notice something about a person she encounters along the way. It can be the smallest thing, like earrings or their hairstyle. Whatever it is, Anna will notice and mention it, and you can see the person's face light up when they hear her words. You can see their body language change because they feel unique and special. They aren't just another person in the Starbucks line. They matter.

Anna's talent is amazing to watch. She notices, communicates, and connects with others in person or on a video call like it's second nature. And the person feels valued and understood on a human level.

This humanity forges a connection that makes a sale more likely, but that's not why Anna does it. She is genuinely interested in others, and authentic connection is important to her. In fact, it's one of her core values.

JUST ONE MORE SALE

You've probably experienced the opposite of authentic connection on a sales call. You're trying to listen to the salesman, let's call him Peter. You are interested in buying the thing he's selling, or you wouldn't have gotten on the call. But you feel icky, like you're being pushed into a corner. You can't wait to get off the line and go take a shower.

Why is that?

There are two reasons. One, the call felt like a giant transaction. Peter obviously doesn't see you as a human being. His goal is not to support you. His goal is to sell you something, so he's more interested in his pitch than your reality.

The second reason might not be obvious: Peter didn't set the stage for what would happen during your time together. He didn't lead you in what you should expect. Because of that, you spent the whole call bracing yourself. And that bracing is natural! It's your body's way of protecting itself. You put up a guard to prepare for the high price tag that was coming. But that wariness isn't something you should feel as a client.

Human desire is simple: we all have the need to be seen, heard, and understood. By establishing rapport, you can meet the other person's deepest need. You will turn discomfort into connection, and transaction into relationship. The client may ultimately choose to work with someone else, but you will help them make that choice wholeheartedly, and you'll feel good about it. So will they.

In this chapter, I'll share how you can make this transition and stop the sales yuck. Forever.

I'm going to teach you how to create a joyous and successful sales conversation with your potential client. I'll show you how to be like Anna and not like Peter. I will teach you how to build rapport, and also how to set a thoughtful intention at the beginning of the call. I will show you why both are necessary, and I'll give you the tools to do both quickly and naturally. And in doing so, you will set yourself up for even greater success.

MORE ABOUT RAPPORT

Let's talk about Anna again. Once, when I was with her at the grocery store, she noticed a crystal necklace that a woman was wearing. She asked her if it had a meaning, and they began talking. They found out that they both did healing and energy work, and they ended up having a deep conversation about that shared experience. In the space of just a few minutes, they had created a connection and a meaningful bond.

Rapport is so much more than asking "How are you?" or "Tell me about your business." Rapport is a mutual trust between parties.

When you get into rapport with someone, it's like walking hand in hand with them. Without rapport, nothing else I teach you will be effective. In this chapter, I'll show you how to build rapport and stop the sales yuck forever. Once you implement what you learn here, you will hear and see a physical shift in the energy of your prospective clients. They'll relax and lean into a heart-centered sales call with you.

Be Prepared

Before you can begin to establish rapport, you need to be well prepared for the call. How you set yourself up is important because the client will make judgments—it's just human nature. Show up on time. Look nice. Make sure your background looks good. Just like a first date, you only get one first impression!

Common Ground

After showing up to the call prepared, you'll need to find common ground with the client. Trust me, it's there! No matter your background, you'll find that you have something in common with every person on this planet.

Mentioning the weather is a great place to start. It's not controversial, and everyone has an opinion. Asking about the weather may seem silly and oversimplified, but it helps the client recognize that you're interested in more than just the sale.

If you are comfortable and can be genuine, you can try Anna's technique during a sales call. Notice something small that identifies the client as a unique individual, ideally something they chose to wear or a special decoration in the background. Then, mention it and build on that connection.

But when in doubt, stay simple and benign. Talk about the weather.

Be Genuine

At one time or another, we've all received a compliment that felt like it had strings attached. The person had an agenda, or they were hiding something. They weren't being genuine, and something just felt off. You didn't want to have anything to do with them after that, did you?

The fact is people can detect your BS in the same way. If you don't feel genuine, or don't truly believe what you're saying, none of the rest matters. So it's essential for you to do the inner work. Make sure what you say feels true. Let your intentions be genuine.

Work on Body Language

According to body language researcher Albert Mehrabian, 55 percent of communication is nonverbal.[2] This means it's essential to host sales calls face-to-face. You and the client will communicate better on video, and this connection will fast-track the decision-making process. Video calls communicate much more than a phone call ever could!

This is why the inner work of sales is so important. The words you say on the call don't matter as much as you think they do. What you communicate through tone, facial expressions, posture, and gestures will ultimately hold the most meaning for the client.

I recommend that you practice your body language, being aware of your facial expressions, the position of your shoulders, and your movements. When you can approach a call from a fully embodied, heart-centered place with natural body language, you allow the client to connect with themselves. This helps them make their decision from their own heart center.

Mirror the Client

When a prospective client is speaking fast and you're speaking slow, it can be subconsciously upsetting for them.

2 "How Much Communication Is Nonverbal?" The University of Texas Permian Basin, accessed September 8, 2022, https://online.utpb.edu/about-us/articles/communication/how-much-of-communication-is-nonverbal/.

Matching the client's pace and body language helps them come back into their embodiment. They will feel more connected and grounded in their own self, and to you. This is another reason why it's critical to have enrollment conversations on video—seeing the other person allows you to match them.

Everyone speaks rhythmically, like a drum, and an excellent way to build rapport with the client is to fall into their drumbeat. Mirror their pace and their tone of voice. If they go high, you go high. If they go low, you do, too. If they're talking fast and they're all over the place, so are you.

Mirroring works with body language as well. When the client crosses their legs, you cross yours. When their arms are open, your arms are open, and when they sit up tall, you follow suit. As human beings, we do this instinctively when we feel connected to the person we're talking with. As coaches, we want to exaggerate that mirroring to demonstrate connection—we truly see the other person, and they see us.

Once you've established a connection, you'll see that the client will start to mimic *you*. At that point, you can slowly and methodically bring them back to your level. For example, if they are talking fast and are all over the place, you mirror them by talking fast, but just long enough to establish rapport. Then bring your tone and pace slowly back to calm. In doing so, you'll see that mirroring is not just a way to build rapport; it's also an easy way to take command of the call.

I want to assure you that mirroring is not deception, manipulation, or trickery. All of us do it in our daily interactions, and as coaches, we do it even when we aren't selling. Working on your mirroring skills simply enhances your brain's ability to do something you already do naturally. Chris Voss, former FBI hostage negotiator and author of *Never Split the Difference: Negotiating As If Your Life Depended Upon It,* has a wonderful MasterClass that highlights mirroring in a beautiful way. Many coaches have refined their mirroring skills by watching his MasterClass and reading his book.

So return to nature. Return to how you would normally act if you could wave a wand and remove the sales energy from your body.

Now let's move on to setting the intention of a call.

ESTABLISH THE INTENTION

Remember when you were a kid and you wanted to play a new game with your friends? If you had never played it before, maybe you were nervous. Maybe everyone else was having fun except for you. Then someone explained the rules. They told you how to play and how you could win. Suddenly, you were able to relax! You could join the game and feel good about it *because you knew what would happen.* In other words, you knew the intention of the game.

An intention for a sales conversation works the same way. The spoken intention serves as a road map for what's going to happen—it functions as a plan of action. It lets you and the client come into agreement about why you're meeting and what you'll do together. If you don't set the intention, the prospective client will be bracing themselves for the worst the entire time. But once they know what will happen, they're able to relax.

Here is how it works. When I begin a sales call, I explain that in the next forty-five minutes we will:

1. Get clear on the client's goals and why they're here.

2. Start to dream about what the future might look like—what they want and how they want to live and work.

3. Then if it feels like a good fit for both of us, I'm happy to share how I work with clients and our next steps moving forward.

Giving the client a road map of what to expect sets the stage for a good call. They understand why I'm asking questions, and what I will do with their answers. They're told in a subtle way that as they're checking me out, I'm checking them out, too. We'll make a mutual determination as to whether or not we should work together.

When I finish giving the other person an idea of what to expect, I pause and ask, "Does this feel good to you?" They always say yes, and this first yes begins a pattern of many yeses. They agree to answer my questions and to communicate and connect.

Another benefit of setting the intention is that it creates a mini-partnership within the conversation. It's neat because instead of showing off your coaching skills by coaching on the call, you demonstrate what it's like to hold space for them. You give them a preview of the beautiful client-coach partnership they'll experience when you work together.

And intentions don't just apply to sales calls, by the way. They apply to every part of life. Think of how you can be more intentional in all your conversations with others. How can you share your intention for any given meeting and what you hope to receive at the end? How can you welcome the intentions of others?

COMING BACK TO YOUR HEART CENTER

Now that you know how to establish rapport and set the intention, it's time for you to practice having these conversations. I recommend practicing first and foremost with clients on actual enrollment calls. Consciously implement these techniques on your next call and monitor how it goes. What went well? What could you do better next time?

With practice, you'll rewire your brain's neural pathways, and these conversations will become second nature to you. You'll put your feet on the floor and monitor your breathing. You'll effortlessly come back to your body and breath over and over again. Adding femininity into the sales conversation will, over time, come to you more and more easily.

While I may have taught you how to show up to a sales call, what's more important is *who* you are when you show up. What's your intention? Are you showing up as yourself? Can you view this potential client as a human being? Do you want to help them more than you want to make the sale?

If you can make this shift in your mind and heart, everything else will fall into place.

THE LIES CLIENTS TELL

I WAS ON A SALES CALL WITH A PROSPECTIVE CLIENT who was seeking support for her business, and outwardly, it seemed to be going fine. She had an amazing job, an advanced degree, and a great family life. But I could tell in my heart that she was holding back. Something was off; there was something she wasn't telling me.

Near the end of our call, I paused, then said, "I have to tell you, it seems to me that you have it all together. Your home and work life appear to be going pretty well. Typically, people don't reach out if everything in their life is perfect. May I have your permission to lean in a bit?"

"Um, yes, go ahead," she replied.

"You seem to have it all together, but I suspect there's a reason why you're on this call today. There's something you're not sharing with me. I'm willing to bet that you present yourself to the world just as you are on this call. You appear to be perfect, and everyone thinks that everything's okay. But it isn't. Tell me where I'm wrong."

Her shoulders relaxed and she exhaled deeply. After what felt like forever, she said quietly, "You're totally right. How did you know? I'm on the brink of a divorce."

"People usually don't hire me if their life is truly put together."

She nodded, and I waited.

"Heck, well, I have to enroll in your program right now!" she said. "You *see* me."

Notice what I did there? I used my coaching language and asked for permission to observe the client more deeply. And I was careful to make space for her to say that I was wrong in my assessment.

The client didn't give any verbal cues indicating that something was wrong. None of the words she used pointed to a problem. It was all in her body language. It was in the monotone she used when she was speaking, and it was in all the things she *didn't* say. (Yet another benefit of hosting video calls.)

By observing this woman's body language and looking for other cues, I was able to better understand her and ask the right questions. We were able to understand the real reason why she wanted coaching. By asking those questions, I was able to share how I could help her with her *real* problem. And in this chapter, I'll teach you how to do this too!

UNCOVERING THE REAL PROBLEM

This client is far from alone; in fact, clients often come to sales calls with a socially acceptable problem—not their *real* problem. The client in this story reached out seeking business support, when in fact, she had a different problem.

Often, I see coaches (particularly female coaches) hesitate to lean into a prospective client's pain. They don't want to "twist the knife" where a person may be struggling the most. They don't want to scare them, and they don't want to lose the sale. But by showing the client you're comfortable with difficult conversations, you demonstrate your depth. Not just as a coach, but as a human being.

As coaches, we have to be really curious. Use your incredible coaching skills to ask thoughtful questions. Show the person that you genuinely care about what's going on in their life. Use your engaged listening skills and watch their body language to uncover the true challenge they are facing, because the prospect may not even be consciously aware of it yet.

The client in the previous story may never have admitted to herself that she was on the brink of a divorce. She may have never subconsciously or verbally said those words. This is why it's such a loving service to lean into the client's struggle. By asking them to reveal the truth to you, you guide them to understand that truth within themselves. Where do they truly need support?

Here are a few questions you can ask to help you understand a client's challenge. You will discover many more questions to ask in each specific situation as you listen.

- "I know it can be hard to talk about, but I'm curious to know, where are you struggling the most right now?"

- "I want us to understand the real reason why you reached out to me. What's working for you lately? What isn't?"

- "What's your biggest area of frustration or challenge?"

- "Of all the difficulties going on in your life/ business, which one feels the heaviest?"

THE TRUTH ABOUT THEMSELVES

Galileo once said, "All truths are easy to understand once they are discovered. The point is to discover them." I love that quote. The most important thing for you to discover is the client's *real problem*. Without that, you won't know what you're talking about, and you won't know how to best support them.

It's important to help clients come to the truth about how they're feeling and what they're facing. But do this gently! In the previous example, I opened the door, but I left space for correction. "This is what I'm seeing. Tell me where I'm wrong." If I missed the mark, I wanted to know.

A client may not want to admit their problem. It may not feel socially acceptable to talk about it. But until you understand what's really going on, the person will never sign. And can you blame them? Why would they pay you to solve a problem that's not the real problem? You can't help them if you don't understand.

NOT AFRAID

On sales calls, I often hear prospective clients say something that at first sounds like it may not be a big deal, or it's not the reason they want to invest in coaching. But if I notice that the client is mentioning that same thing multiple times during a call, I will ask about it to see if something deeper is there. Often, there is. We'll discuss how to go about asking these questions in the next section.

Coaches are more observant because we've never been personally involved in a relationship with the client. We don't have any previous experience with the person to tint our vision. We don't have any motivation to avoid the truth. Parents want to keep family units together. Friends want to have a comfortable conversation. But coaches get right to the heart of it. We identify that stuff because it's our job.

When you stand in the muck with a client during that first sales conversation, you're showing that you're not afraid. You can handle difficult conversations. You can handle discomfort. You are there to support them, and they can be fully present and honest about what they're actually feeling without worrying about your reaction.

THE FOUNDATIONAL STEP

Uncovering the prospective client's true problem is foundational to coaching and essential when selling. You cannot successfully sell without understanding the client's actual problem. Here's an example that shows how thoughtful questions can help you uncover the client's true desires and actual problem on a sales call:

Prospective Client: I want to grow my business.

Coach: What about growing your business is most important to you?

Prospective Client: Well, I don't have enough time for my kids, and I think if I can just get the business to $2 million, I'll have the capacity to hire a full-time CEO and I won't have to work as much day-to-day.

Coach: Sounds like your family and work/life balance are really important to you.

Prospective Client: Yes, they are. And my kids are the reason I started my business in the first place. I wanted to be at home with them.

Coach: Seems like being present for your kids is a value of yours that is nonnegotiable.

Prospective Client: Yes, 100 percent.

Coach: Do you mind if I lean in a bit and share what I often see?

Prospective Client: Sure, of course.

Coach: So I often work with clients who believe that when they finally do the thing they've been wanting to do, or when their business hits seven figures, they'll be able to relax and live the life of their dreams. This is rarely the case. Your kids are growing up quickly, and based on what you've shared, creating a work/life balance is essential. Not when your business is at $2 million but today.

Prospective Client: You're so right. I need help. I'm exhausted. I don't know if I can keep doing this.

Coach: I get it. It sounds like this is going to be a big part of our coaching partnership. We need to help you uncover hidden stressors in your day-to-day life. We need to start making small shifts internally, so you can make big changes with your business and be there for your family.

Prospective Client: Yes! This is what I need. I don't want to keep living this way.

By getting curious, you can get to the heart of the matter, not just the surface level problem. Uncovering the transformation the person truly wants to achieve puts you in a position to help them. This is the goal of coaching, after all. It's also the goal of the sales conversation: to uncover the desired transformation so you can help another human being move forward.

THE COSTS OF INACTION

Let's say you're on a sales call, and you're at the point where you and the prospective client have both come to an understanding of their true pain and struggle. The client sees the choice they need to make, and it's time to help them understand what will happen if they don't make that choice and allow their struggle to continue.

Ask the following:

"Why is it important for you to solve this problem now? What impact is it having on your life/business? What happens if this problem still exists one, two, or even five years from now?"

These questions help in two ways. First, it helps you understand how serious the client is about change. Second, the client begins to understand what they're facing. They need to understand and feel the pain of inaction so they can make a choice.

For example, if a prospective client is complaining about being passed over for a raise, you'll pause to help them understand the cost.

The conversation might look something like this:

You: What was the amount of that raise you missed out on?

Prospective Client: $25,000.

You: Wow. How many years have you missed out on that raise?

Prospective Client: Three years.

You: That's $75,000. That's a really big deal.

Even if you aren't in business coaching, helping the client realize the cost of inaction is still relevant to you. It's truly important for *both* you and the client to understand the full cost of their problem. I can't emphasize this enough.

To give another example, if a client is going to marriage counseling, how much is that costing them? Let's say it's $150 a week. Then they have to pay a babysitter so they can attend their counseling sessions. That's another $60 a week. So that's $840 a month. How much does that cost them per year? More than ten grand!

As a coach, it's your job to help the client understand their true problem and the cost of staying stuck. This gives them space to come to the realization that doing nothing is a very real choice, too. In this case, choosing to stay where they are will continue to cost them more than $10,000 per year.

Discussing the costs of inaction not only helps the client assess the choices in front of them, but it also lets you talk about money before you *need* to talk about money (the investment they would make to work with you). Grounding the problem in terms of money early on helps the client and the conversation in a couple of ways. First, you prevent the money bomb from hitting them at the end without warning. Second, you prepare their brain to be settled and comfortable when it comes to talking about money.

To illustrate this point, let's say I'm on a call with the prospective client who is in marriage counseling, talking about a relationship program that costs $5,000. If they hear that number out of the blue, it will sound like a lot of money. They might immediately tell me they can't afford it. But if we take a step back and I remind them that they're currently paying over $10,000 a year for a solution that isn't working, they begin to understand the true value of entering into a client-coach partnership.

Without putting that $5,000 in context, it's an arbitrarily high amount of money. But once they have something to compare that cost to, it makes more sense. Doing nothing has a real cost. This is why you want to talk about money before you formally talk about money and the investment of coaching.

Only then can a client truly make a choice from their heart center.

HOW TO IDENTIFY A MISALIGNED CLIENT (BEFORE YOU SIGN)

We've already discussed the cost of enrolling a misaligned client, but I'm going to talk about it again. I can't emphasize enough how much they will drain you emotionally, physically, and financially, and how they will detrimentally impact your coaching community. To help you avoid signing on misaligned clients, let's talk about how to identify them before you sign.

Before we get into this, I want you to know that you can do everything right on a sales call, and there will still be times when you won't be able to identify a misaligned client in advance. They may seem good at first, only to reveal their true colors down the line. But with others, you *can* tell. Something about them will feel "off," which tells you they aren't a good fit right at the beginning.

If you are thoughtful, you can identify a bad fit early on and get them off the call. In doing so, you can save yourself and the prospective client a lot of time and trouble.

Red Flags

There are some general questions you should ask yourself about clients when hosting sales calls. For instance:

- Are they coachable?

- Can they accept feedback?

- Do they pay attention to cues?

- Is their personality a good fit for yours?

- Are they kind, or are they off-putting?

- Do you feel a connection?

- Will you look forward to seeing them every week?

These questions will help you decide whether or not you want to work with a prospective client, but you can also look for specific red flags. I recommend gently releasing clients from the call if they display any of the following traits.

Victim Mentality

A victim mentality is a big red flag. I know that when a potential client is blaming their mother, their spouse, their finances, or their boss for their problems, I'll be the next one on their list.

When I hear blaming, my mind stops. Then I ask thoughtful questions designed to show me how deeply this habit of blaming goes. Is a victim mentality a deeply rooted problem in their lives, or are they able to shrug it off when lightly challenged? To find out, I typically ask them to share more about their complaints and inquire as to what they've done to improve the situation. If they've done nothing, what do they think needs to be done? If they continue to blame others and never take responsibility, or if they aren't committed to creating a shift, I will gently release them from the call. Trust yourself in this situation. Trust the signals your brain sends to you, and don't work with a misaligned client. Ever.

One final note here. "You don't know what you don't know," and the only way to learn is to "fail your way forward." You're going to mess up, and occasionally, you'll enroll misaligned clients. Forgive yourself and send them back into the universe with love and gratitude for the gift they provided to you: a lesson learned.

Mental Health Needs

Many coaches shy away from prospective clients who are seeing a psychologist, but I do not. If a client is seeing a psychologist, typically, it's fine to coach them. In fact, coaching and therapy can work beautifully in tandem. The mental health care profession is amazing, and many coaches work in collaboration with psychologists, but our role is to coach, not to provide therapy or diagnoses. The International Coaching Federation (ICF) has great resources if you need further help understanding the differences between coaching and therapy, as well as articulating this difference to clients. It's very important to have clear expectations and boundaries with clients from the moment you enroll them into a partnership with you.

Looking for Somebody to Fix Them

When someone has purchased multiple programs, or they've hired coach after coach after coach, I consider it a definite red flag. If a prospective client jumps from one program to another, it usually means they're looking for external fixes and are unwilling to do the inner work.

To be clear, coaches do not fix people. We don't even give them answers! Instead, we thoughtfully help them come to their own choices and decisions; we serve as guides as the client does their own work.

Disrespect for Boundaries

Some people are very needy, and others habitually push the limits. Regardless of the reason why, it's never worth enrolling someone who won't respect the boundaries I draw around the client-coach partnership. Never disregard the signs of a boundary-pusher. Here are a few examples:

- Showing up late to sales calls

- Rescheduling sales calls at the last minute

- Multitasking during a sales call

- Requesting heavily modified payment plans

- Asking you to modify your offer to the extreme

- Asking you to coach differently

A "Prove It" Mentality

Some clients come to a sales call demanding proof. They ask things like, "What's your success rate?" or "How do I know this will work?" Both of these questions seem legit on the surface, and the client isn't wrong to ask. But the truth is that I don't know if coaching will work for them. The only guarantee I have is that if they show up and do the work, *something* will change.

Aligned clients are looking for guides or support. Misaligned clients often look for someone to fix or cure them in some way, and they want a guarantee that they will be cured. Someone who has a "prove it" mentality is rarely a good client.

You'll come to recognize other red flags as you host more calls and gain more experience. Some of those flags, like the ones referenced here, will be general and apply across the board, and others will be specific to you.

Check Your Biases

You may think that you have no biases, but that's simply not true. All of us have implicit biases (ones we aren't consciously aware of), and they can have a negative influence when it comes to determining whether or not a client is a good fit for your program.

To give some examples, you may be on a sales call with a potential client who doesn't look, act, or dress like you, and you might conclude early on that the two of you aren't aligned. Maybe their sense of humor differs from yours, they speak with an accent, or they're a different race or gender. Maybe they're younger or older than your typical client, and that leads you to decide they aren't a fit.

It's so important for you to not let these factors play into your decision. If you feel that biases may be influencing you during a sales call, do a gut check. Be extra thoughtful in the questions you ask and take more time to understand the client and their background. You'll be so glad you did!

THE HIDDEN COSTS

I'm asking you to trust me as I repeat this unfortunate truth. If you enroll someone in your program who's not a good fit, no matter how much the client pays for your program, it will still cost you three times as much in time and energy, and you'll have less of an impact on your other clients. A bad fit will inevitably make you question your ability as a coach. It may even lead you to question your desire to continue with your business altogether.

When you say no to the clients who display red flags, you say yes to other things. You say yes to allowing the right people to energize you. You say yes to creating the right environment in your coaching programs. You say yes to fostering connection, rapport, positivity, and inspiration. You say yes to all the things that people want from coaching.

By saying no to the wrong client, you protect your heart. You protect your energy. And you actually do the client a service, because it's likely that circumstances will steer them in the right direction.

THE CLIENT'S TRUE DESIRE

IN THE LAST CHAPTER, I SHOWED YOU HOW TO UNCOVER a client's true problem. You also learned the importance of talking about money and how to discuss the true cost of staying stuck. Now that you know how to help the client identify their real problem, how do you tap into what they truly *want*?

When you know what a client truly desires, you can show how you would help them take aligned action toward their goal. You're able to explain what the next steps might look like. Tapping into the client's true desire through an embodiment exercise is essential for a successful sales conversation.

EMBODIED DECISIONS

What is embodiment? I'm sure you've heard the term "embodiment" before, and I've mentioned it several times already, but what does it really mean? It's a term commonly used in holistic practice, yoga, and many coaching fields. But not every coach will be familiar with what it means. Let's take a minute to define it.

I like this definition from *Positive Psychology*: "Embodiment practices use the body as a tool for healing through self-awareness, mindfulness, connection, self-regulation, finding balance, and creating self-acceptance. Embodiment explores the relationship between our physical being and our energy."[3]

The Somatic Movement Project explains it in a slightly different way. "An embodiment practice is a method of using unique sensations of our body as a tool to develop awareness, stay present, self-regulate, feel whole, find balance, feel connected, know oneself, love oneself, and be empowered."[4]

Using embodiment practices during a sales call helps you do just that. You stay aware. You feel present and whole. And you want your clients to feel all these sensations as well! Their experience is guided by you. Their feelings, their sensations, and the start of the client-coach partnership originates with *you*.

---

3 Melissa Madeson, "Embodiment Practices: How to Heal Through Movement," PositivePsychology.com, August 11, 2021, https://positivepsychology.com/embodiment-philosophy-practices/.

4 "What Is an Embodiment Practice?" Somatic Movement Project, accessed September 8, 2022, https://somatic-movement-project.com/why-cultivate-a-somatic-practice/.

THE BODY SHOWS THE WAY

Studies show that people know whether or not they want to date someone within seconds of meeting them.[5] You read that correctly. *Within seconds*! They meet someone who appeals to their emotion, and emotion is the leader. It's only after they feel the emotion that they go to their brain to validate what their body is feeling.

So, what does this statistic tell us? It tells us that, contrary to popular belief, our decisions are not made logically; they're made emotionally. Which decisions are made emotionally, you ask? *All of them*. Including purchasing decisions.[6]

If people make decisions emotionally, this should change the way you do sales, right? After all, if people don't make decisions logically, there's no point in trying to appeal to them by telling them about the logical benefits in your offer. It's a waste of breath.

Decisions are made through the power of the body, not the brain. When it comes to connecting and helping a client feel into the choice they want to make, you need to help them go within. They have to tune into their heart space to find what

5   Kelly Gonsalves, "Is Love at First Sight Real? Why It Happens & 9 Signs You're Experiencing It," mbgrelationships, July 31, 2021, https://www.mindbodygreen.com/articles/love-at-first-sight/.

6   Michael Harris, "Neuroscience Confirms We Buy on Emotion & Justify with Logic & Yet We Sell to Mr. Rational & Ignore Mr. Intuitive," CustomerThink, April 2, 2017, https://customerthink.com/neuroscience-confirms-we-buy-on-emotion-justify-with-logic-yet-we-sell-to-mr-rational-ignore-mr-intuitive/#.

they truly desire. This can only happen if a parasympathetic response occurs in their body.

Most people are familiar with the sympathetic nervous system response, commonly known as "fight or flight," which occurs when the body is under stress. The stressor can range from something minor, like being stuck in traffic, to something major, like being chased by a bear. The fight or flight response increases heart rate, blood pressure, and sweating. It also causes the pupils to dilate, and the body will be on high alert. You do not want your client in this sympathetic state during a sales call.

An embodiment exercise helps the prospective client have the opposite, parasympathetic response of "rest and digest" to come to their decision. With this response, the heart rate decreases, and muscles relax. When the client is in a parasympathetic state, they calm down and feel safe and supported. They can self-regulate and find balance, and it's from this place of deep calm and peace that they can make decisions from their innermost self, rather than from scarcity or fear. They can get out of their heads and into their hearts.

It's from this space that the client can step into what they truly desire, not what they *think* they should do. It's from this space that they can identify what they truly want. Not what their mother wants. Not what their spouse wants. Not what their boss or anyone else wants. What *they* want. And it's from this space that we start to eliminate the *shoulds*:

I should make money.

I should be a good mom.

I should.

I should.

And I should, again.

Thoughtfully using your coaching skills and helping your client go within helps them get to the root of their deepest desires. Everyone wants to identify what they truly desire, and an embodiment exercise can help uncover this. I've seen its efficacy on hundreds and hundreds of sales calls.

Using an embodiment exercise before you ask a client about their vision reaches into the part of their brain that has been hiding. Their brain has most likely been putting everything and everyone else first for a long time, and an embodiment exercise looks into the part of the brain that is their body and soul. Encourage clients to quiet down, put both feet on the floor, place their hands on their hearts, and take a deep breath to expand their vision beyond the goals they *should* set.

Before I used a formal embodiment exercise on a sales call, clients gave me simple answers to the questions I asked about their goals. They wanted to grow their business. They wanted to stay married, or to keep their job. A common refrain was: "I just want to pay the bills and be happy, you know?"

When I began doing embodiment exercises before asking these questions, everything changed! I created a safe space. I led people through to their vision. Many of my clients commented that they'd never been treated this way on a sales call—ever. They'd never been invited to go inward. They'd never been guided and encouraged to think bigger.

It's incredible what people say on the other side of embodiment. Some will even reveal things they've never said to another human being before.

People say they want to shut down a business, leave a relationship, or leave a job. Others will find a vision for the future they've never had before. "I want to have a marriage that's amazing and fulfilling and lights me up!" "I want to have a job that recognizes my value. I'm not okay with getting passed up for a raise anymore."

People surprise themselves when they become embodied. They become *clear*. They desire more than they've ever dared to dream. And they want to get there.

You Can't Be Serious

I know what's going on in your head right now. You're thinking, "You can't be serious. No way is a prospective client going to close their eyes, get centered, and come into their heart space." I used to think the same thing.

The fact is, you don't lead a client through an embodiment exercise because it sounds nice and feels good. You do it because it's incredibly effective and supports the client in making their decision. While the exercise can feel awkward at first, doing so will make you stand out in your profession. The result of an embodiment exercise is an exciting experience that creates an internal shift for your client. It doesn't matter if you're a copywriter, business coach, accountant, or life coach. Embodiment exercises can lead to results that will blow your clients away! Simply modify the exercise to fit your clientele and be prepared for your clients to be surprised and delighted at this request.

FALLING SHORT

I've noticed that the prospective client's answers to my questions fall short when I skip the embodiment exercise. When I ask the client about their goals without first helping them go within, I get mediocre answers that just focus on survival.

No one invests in high-priced coaching to survive. They do it to thrive! And to get them there, I bring people through an embodiment exercise. That's when the client says things that blow both their mind and mine. It's when the client lights up and says a resounding yes to the program.

They're so excited about the possibilities. They didn't know they wanted to write that book or leave their marriage. Or they didn't know they wanted to save their marriage or buy the business. They never allowed themselves to fully admit to that desire. But when they realize their desire, it's a magic moment.

That's the peak, and the peak is where you transition: you invite them to work with you. This is one of the best parts of the conversation.

When you help a client tune into their heart's desire, the vision they will get will blow your mind. Not only will they be excited to work with you, but you'll be excited to work with them, too!

COMING BACK TO HEART CENTER

So how do you do this, exactly? How do you get your prospective client out of their head and into their heart? One of my mentors, Laura Wieck, taught me how to formally insert an embodiment exercise into a sales call. Here's an approach that works.

First, you break rapport. I know, I taught you how to create rapport in a previous chapter, but in this situation, you deliberately want to break it. An easy way to do this is by saying the client's name.

On sales calls, clients often ramble and tell you about all their problems. Maybe they're blaming other people, maybe they aren't, but at some point, you help them come back to the here and now. You'll say their name, once, twice, or three times. "Sarah. Sarah. Sarah." They'll pause and look up.

Then you invite them to return to their body. Here are a couple of examples of how to guide them:

- "Sarah, let's help you get out of your head. Let's put all that stuff aside and tune in to what it is that you truly desire."

- "Hey, we've really been up in our heads about all the things we want to accomplish. There are so many goals. Let's set that aside and come into our heart space for a minute."

These sentences will redirect your client completely. You've asked for permission, and you've both put everything aside. Now you're in command of the conversation.

Ask the client to take a few deep breaths. Ask them to put their feet on the floor, and you'll do it, too. Then close your eyes for a second. Put your hand on your heart and take a deep breath. Your client will join. When you sigh, they will sigh.

Then you will walk them through the embodiment exercise of your choice.

The goal of whatever embodiment exercise you select is to help your client visualize what their life could be like. "Don't think about what you should do, or what anybody else wants you to do. What's in your heart? What is at your core? What do you dream of?" Once you and your client find the quiet whisper that drives them, encourage them to go deeper. What will stepping into their desires look and feel like?

Then ask them this very important question: "Why now? Why is it important to step into this *now*?"

THE REVELATION

When a revelation occurs following an embodiment exercise, it isn't always dramatic, though sometimes it can be. But one thing's for sure: there's almost always a shift. This is true for both sales calls and coaching calls, and I use this exercise during both. Let's go through an example from a coaching call.

Perhaps a client starts out wanting to hire three more people for their business. But after the embodiment exercise, the idea of three more people feels exhausting. He still wants to grow his business, but that action feels so *heavy*.

Great. He's identified that hiring three more people isn't his true desire. So I ask him, "What might another option be?"

"Well, we could do Plan B. That's so big and risky, though. Hiring three people just feels safer."

Then, we dig into whether or not Plan B might be the way.

Now, once we dig in, it's not as if everything changes all at once. Humans are wired for survival, not success. We're wired to be cavemen—we believe we're meant to build fires and just survive day by day. However, the embodiment and vision exercises help clients put survival, fear, and today's circumstances to the side. It allows them to begin thinking about building empires or turning big dreams into reality.

We all have a fire inside of us, and we know there's more. But the weight of everyday life keeps us treading water. Embodiment helps people dream bigger and start to create the life they desire. And that feels *fantastic*, for both you and the client.

GET YOUR HANDS OUT OF OTHER PEOPLE'S POCKETS

YEARS AGO, I WORKED AS A NONPROFIT FUNDRAISER for a world-class health care institution. I went to former patients' homes, sat in their living rooms, and heard about their experiences with the organization. Then I asked them for a large sum of money as a donation. If they gave, these people would be helping others through the same organization that had helped them.

One day, I was asked to meet with a woman who was visiting the institution. She was a farmer, so she lived out in the country. She drove a Honda Accord that was covered in muck from constantly driving on dirt roads. If I had met her anywhere else, I never would have thought she could make the kind of donation I usually asked for.

Still, I followed the systems and the structure I had put in place for myself. I approached her like I would a friend. I continued to nurture her. She was an amazing human being, and I was thankful for the opportunity to connect with her.

The second time I met with her, we went out to lunch and had a conversation about her experience with the institution. And then I presented the opportunity. "Based on what you've shared with me," I said, "it seems like the institution has had an incredible impact on your life. Would you consider making a gift to the department that supported you?"

Without hesitation, she told me yes.

"Great. What amount would feel good to you? What amount would feel equal to the amount of care and support that you've received?"

This kind woman paused for a minute. Then she looked up with a smile. "I think about a million dollars."

I choked on my salad a bit. Then I got it together. "Wonderful, then. Lunch is on me!"

From that day on, I checked my bias with every single call and in every single conversation.

YOU CAN'T TELL
BY LOOKING

Not every person who appears to be poor is poor. Many people live modestly but have piles of money stacked under their mattress. They drive simple cars, and you'd never guess that they're loaded. Then you have people who live in expensive zip codes and drive luxury automobiles. They look like they have it all together, when in reality they're just a payment away from losing everything.

You can't tell how much money a person does or does not have by looking at them.

Imagine if I had judged the woman who made the million-dollar donation based on her car or her appearance. I would have committed theft by judging her. I would have stolen from her by not providing her with the opportunity to make the gift, and she wouldn't have joined the club of donors at this next level. I also would have robbed the people who would go on to benefit from her donation. My judgment or predisposition about what I thought she could or couldn't spend would have deprived her (and others) of the greater good. Who did I think I was to make that call?

The bottom line? Judging is *not* okay.

THE INNER WORK

It's not your job to determine if a prospective client can or can't afford your program in sales conversations. In fact, it's none of your business. Your job is to present them with the opportunity. It's up to you to show them the cost of staying stuck. The client may be richer than you know, or the opportunity may be important enough that they want to spend the money necessary to fix it. The decision is *theirs*.

In the beginning, no one is impartial on sales calls. We make judgments based on what someone is wearing, and even what their background looks like on a video call. I invite you to work toward ignoring those things. Get your hand out of your clients' pockets and do your job. Focus on helping them understand their true problem and find their true desire. Don't waste precious energy trying to figure out what they can or can't afford.

If you take your eyes off the client's true problem and true desire and instead get caught up or make a judgment (in your mind) about their ability to afford your services, you block the client from the important work of *understanding what they need* and coming to a choice on the call.

Sometimes people step into a program knowing it will be a huge financial stretch for them. Maybe they have to reach out to a family member for a loan. Maybe they have to put it on a credit card. But then the program absolutely changes their life forever. Who am I to decide if they should take the risk?

Who am I to question their decisions? What they choose to do with their money is absolutely none of my business.

So, how do you get past your judgments and fears? How do you look past what someone is wearing? How do you stop making assumptions about what others can or can't afford? One way is through experience, and I'll share some of mine with you in this chapter. For some coaches, that will be enough. Others may have to learn the hard way.

I've had a client tell me on a sales call that she was about to lose her house, and then she paid in full fifteen minutes later. Another client had $100 in her bank account, but she found a way to make it happen. Sure, it was painful for them to pay for a high-priced coaching program, but they chose to enroll anyway. What's the key takeaway here?

It turns out that *money is not a real objection.*

I understand that Americans don't usually have open discussions about money. And the people who do talk about money freely are usually the ones who don't have it. It's okay to talk about being poor or to say that you don't have money. But it's not okay to talk about having it. We fail to realize that we have an incredibly intimate relationship with money, whether we have abundant financial resources or not. Your house, the furniture in it, and the furnace that keeps it warm all cost money. Everything around you costs money. Money is flowing everywhere, but we don't respect it. We blame and resent it. This is where we need to shift our perspective about money.

So if a client says, "I can't afford it," they really mean they don't want to work with you, or they don't see the value in what you're doing. If they say they need to talk to their spouse before they spend the money, it pretty much means the same thing. Use your engaged listening skills on a call to understand a client's true objection, because it's rarely about money.

We figure out a way to afford what we desire, right? Most people can't afford to go to college, but they find a way. They get the loans. They do it because a higher education is what they desire. The inner work of sales centers around getting very, very settled about that truth. Lean into the truth that the objection isn't really about money.

BE NICE TO MONEY!

I encourage you to change the way you talk about money, both to yourself and to others. For example, let's say your mother-in-law asks you if you want to go on a vacation to Hawaii. If you don't want to go, I invite you not to say you can't afford it, but that Hawaii isn't where you choose to vacation this year. You've decided to go to Cancun, or to stay home instead.

Recently, my sister-in-law told me she couldn't afford to go to the movies. What she meant was, "I don't want to go to the movies." She, like so many others, is conditioned to use money as an excuse, and in doing so she doesn't articulate her true desires.

When you lie to yourself about money, even little micro lies, it feels crummy. You feel stuck and you feel small. But when you start thinking and talking about money differently, things will shift for you. You'll show up to your sales calls feeling lighter. It won't take long for this to happen.

The easiest way to shift your mindset is to notice your words. I invite you to start a list on your phone's notepad or in a small notebook. Every time you blame money, whether speaking to yourself or someone else, note it with a small checkmark. Once you notice this, you can start to recondition your neural pathways to believe that different choices are possible.

Next, you'll want to notice how you verbally communicate. Let's say you and I just talked about coaching. You seemed interested, so I invited you to join a program. You said you couldn't afford it, but in reality, you choose not to enroll right now. If you had wanted it, you would have found a way; it's just not your highest priority. Other things are more important to you, and you should articulate that, rather than placing the blame on money.

Now, maybe you really can't afford, say, a $5 million house. You truly cannot, there's no way! But generally, you make decisions day-to-day about things you *can* afford, but choose not to buy or do. You blame money because it's a nice scapegoat. You say you can't take that trip to Hawaii with your mother-in-law because you can't afford it, when the truth is, you're choosing not to, and you don't want to admit that you've made that choice.

We can't let go of all our habits all at once, so I'm just asking for you to start wiggling the tooth. Start speaking the truth about money and your choices and see how your mindset begins to change.

CHANGE HOW YOU SPEAK TO PROSPECTIVE CLIENTS

You're on a sales call, and a prospective client tells you they can't afford coaching. What do you say? Since we now know that money isn't really an objection, how do you invite the client to talk about their *real* objection to working with you?

During these conversations, don't assume what the client can or can't afford. Start thinking and talking about money differently. When you can speak the truth both internally and externally, you will see a shift happen very quickly.

If this seems difficult, don't worry. In Chapter 10, I'll tell you exactly what to say when a client says, "I can't afford it." But the first step to supporting your client in coming to a choice is a shift in *your* mindset.

SET YOUR (MONEY) BAGGAGE ASIDE

We all have an intimate relationship with money. It's present in nearly every aspect of our lives. Even though we don't generally acknowledge the impact our parents had on how we approach money, our thoughts about money originate from them. How our parents talked about and treated money has a great influence on us. If they painted a negative picture of money, now is the time to change that inner dialogue. Yes, you can begin a new relationship with money!

You should come to sales calls as a blank slate. Don't bring your past money baggage to the call. Your childhood experiences will encumber you, and you need to be fully present.

Fortunately for me, my fundraising jobs got me very comfortable with talking about money. I talked about it openly and freely on a daily basis, and in doing so, it became a part of me. To this day, I may talk about money in a "socially inappropriate" way over dinner with friends. I'll ask them how much commission they made on the sale of a house, how much money they raised for a charity, or how much they expect to receive for a bonus this year. My husband always says this makes him uncomfortable, but I still ask, because I have a healthy relationship with money, and I want to celebrate financial wins with others.

This is why the internal work of sales is essential. When you get right with money, everything else gets easier.

EXERCISES TO IMPROVE YOUR RELATIONSHIP WITH MONEY

So far in this chapter, I've talked about changing your mindset about money. I know this is easier said than done, so I've provided some exercises to help you along this part of the journey.

1. Take a minute to think about your predispositions around sales and money. How did your family spend money? What's the narrative behind that?

Here are a few questions to help you think about your family history and your subsequent money story:

- How did your parents talk about money?

    * Did they think in terms of lack or abundance?

    * Did they spend or did they save?

    * Did they blame money or use money as a scapegoat?

    * Was it okay to talk about costs and dollar amounts or was it taboo?

- If you have a spouse, how do the two of you handle money?

    * Do either of you need to get "permission" before you make a buying decision?

    * Do you have separate or combined bank accounts?

* Do you use credit cards?

* Are you comfortable with debt?

To give an example, I'll share my own background with money. I've always considered my parents to be the richest poor people I've ever met. They've always thought they could afford anything. I ask them how, and they shrug. "We don't know, we just sign up. We do it. We know we'll figure it out." And they do. They're always in a place of expansive possibilities. They say yes to the things they want, and no to the things they don't want, easily and without guilt. They cut spending on things that don't matter so they can say yes to other things that light them up. Their life is rich and abundant, even though they aren't rich. It's a nice way to live.

Now, my best friend's parents are different. They always have money in the bank, but they're conservative with it. They save and plan and make "responsible" buying decisions. They value stability and fairness and take fewer risks. This is the way they choose to handle their money, and they too have created a rich and abundant life for themselves.

I want you to know that your parents' story is not yours. *You* get to decide how to talk to money, how you feel about it, and the type of relationship you're going to have with it. There's no right or wrong—people simply have different mindsets about money. So the first step to showing up to a sales call with a blank slate is to identify your current money mindset, and then consciously choose the mindset you'll have going forward.

2. Once you've considered your family history with money, return to the exercise I suggested earlier in this chapter and make a checkmark every time you blame money for something you don't want to do. Try this for at least one week.

Every time you blame money, whether on the spot or later that day, consider what you said. Is it really 100 percent true that you couldn't afford that thing? Is it true only under certain circumstances? Could you really not afford to go out to dinner or did you just prefer to spend your money on something else? Is it really money's "fault"?

3. Given that you're in an intimate relationship with money, how do you want to treat it? How do you want to speak to it? Make a list of the ways you want to show up in this relationship. Start with "I love money and money loves me."

Don't blame money for the choices you make. When you're mean to money it will be mean to you. But when you speak kindly to money and treat it appropriately, you show up to your sales calls ready to receive, and you will receive in abundance.

I love coaching others in this area. If you do the work and question your thinking about money, you can move past blame. It doesn't take long, and you can live a happier life because of it. You can view money for what it truly is—something that comes and goes and is there to serve you.

This shift changes *everything*.

THE TRUTH

Money is a renewable resource, but time is not. You can never make more time, but you can always make more money.

For the healers and feelers reading this book, you may have been conditioned to believe that people who have money are evil. You may believe they do bad things and hurt other people, all for the sake of making money. Yes, some people are like that! But there are many others like the woman who made the large donation over lunch. She took a million dollars and gave it to people in need.

The only way money can work is if it's exchanged. Otherwise, it has no value. If money just sits in an account, it does nobody any good. The exchange of money expands its value for everyone.

As a coach, it's important to show up to coaching sessions without predispositions about what people can or can't afford. And you have to do the same thing with money in general. Investigate, think about, and contemplate your money story. Let go of your biases and the parts of your relationship with money that don't serve you.

EMBRACING FREEDOM

Many coaches offer entire programs designed to address money mindsets, and for good reason. When you can free yourself and stop blaming money, your possibilities will expand.

So what's your mindset about money right now? Going forward, how are you going to talk about money? How will you teach your kids to talk about money? What do you want your relationship with money to look like?

When you break the hold that money has over you, you can make a conscious decision to keep making progress on your journey. You can show up to your sales calls ready to receive!

TAKE THE MONEY, HONEY!

ABOUT A YEAR AGO, I DECIDED TO MAKE A REALLY BIG investment in my business. I had contemplated it. I had talked with others. I had read and studied about it. This program was the best, so I scheduled a call with a salesperson, Dan.

By the way, I was all in before I even scheduled the call. I had already made the decision to enroll. Or so I thought.

I had traveled across the country to teach a live workshop, and I took time out of the event to talk to Dan. I found a little nook in the corner of the conference room and settled in for the call. I was nervous and excited. Dan was great, and we had a wonderful conversation.

At the end, I told him, "This is a yes for me. What are my next steps?"

He said, "Here's what I'll do. I'm going to send you a contract. Look it over and sign when you're ready."

He sent it, but I didn't sign.

Two weeks went by, and I continued to interview people who had been through the program. I was up every night thinking about it. I stared at the ceiling, questioning whether or not I should join. I read every article, blog post, and review I could find. I listed out success rates to help justify my decision.

I will never, ever get those two weeks of my life back. Ever! And the worst part? None of my fretting was necessary.

Had Dan hosted a video call, he would have seen that I literally had my credit card out, ready to go. If he would have charged me, say, $1,000 on the spot, a tiny fraction of the price of the program, the decision would have been made right then and there. I would have taken the initial step, and I wouldn't have lost two weeks of sleep. In the end, I enrolled, but only because he had the best game in town. And unless you have the best game in town, you won't be so lucky!

Looking back, I'm irritated that he didn't charge me up front. His job as a salesperson was to help me take the next step, both physically and emotionally, but he failed to do so. He didn't know that *the exchange of money is a powerful activator.*

When I take money from my clients during the first sales call, they take action immediately. They go out and hire nannies so they can focus on their businesses. They ask their spouses for support. They quit their jobs. They're ready to do the transformative work.

Think of how many sales Dan loses—people might be right there, ready to go, but they aren't provided with a solid next step. Some of these people are executives, and they're incredibly busy. They don't have time to think about or make this decision multiple times! They also have to use their own time on a different day to put their credit card information into a payment system.

As a salesperson, it's your job to help the client make a decision. When they say yes, you take the money on the spot. Call it an activation fee, and you can make it as small as $500, or as large as $5,000. It doesn't matter. Once you activate their decision, they're off to the races!

Again, *the exchange of money is a powerful activator.* Don't overlook or neglect it.

The Problem with Initial Invoices

Many new coaches reach out to me with excitement when they hear their first yes. Of course, I'm happy for them.

Then I ask if they activated the client-coach partnership with a fee. Oftentimes, they tell me they didn't charge an activation fee, they just sent the client an invoice. And just as often, the coach never hears from that client again.

When you send an initial invoice instead of taking money from a client the moment they say yes, you may think you're doing them a favor, but you aren't. The problem with an invoice is that it leaves the client to their own devices. Or it allows time for work or life to get busy, and they'll never get around to paying it. They'll never get around to scheduling their first coaching call, and they'll just move on.

This is why it's so important to take the money up front. It activates the client's decision, doesn't leave room for their fears to get the better of them, and you're there to support them in their next steps. Taking the money gives them the certainty of crossing that line. As a coach, your job is not only to help a client make a decision, but to help them move boldly forward into action.

OUT OF SIGHT, OUT OF MIND

I used to receive an invoice for $600 each month from a social media company I had hired. This wasn't a big bill, but I saw it every month. And every month I had to ask myself if they had done $600 worth of work. I had to reen-roll myself in that decision constantly. Had the company put me on automatic payments, I never would have noticed. The company's work was just okay, and I felt like managing them was costing me more stress than the $600 bill. Since I had to think about their work every month, I decided to let them go.

Sending recurring bills and invoices forces a client to make their decision over and over again, and that's not nice. You're there to support the client when you're on calls, but you won't be there when they're at home, clicking a button to make a payment. You tell yourself that they will feel more secure if they enter their credit card information themselves, but that's not true. The truth is that it feels more comfortable *to you*.

As a coach and salesperson, it's your job to stand in discomfort with the client from the first sales call, and every week thereafter. If you don't have the chutzpah to stand the slightly uncomfortable situation of taking their credit card information, how will you support them through their divorce? How will you help them work through the loss of family members, illnesses, or other major life events?

What you need to do is simple. Get on the call and activate the yes. Take their money and set up recurring payments each month. This way, you never, ever have to invoice a client. It's a tiny, tiny shift that will make you so much money and help your clients move forward smoothly.

THE PAYMENT PLAN

As you present the cost of your program, take into consider-ation the fact that clients aren't actually buying the price of the program. They're buying the payment plan.

For instance, I don't remember how much my sweet Toyota Sienna costs. It might be $35,000 or maybe $55,000—who knows? What I do know is that I pay $375 a month, and that price feels good to me.

When coaches insist that clients pay in full, they often lose the sale. I know, because I've reviewed dozens of sales calls from coaches who don't understand where they're going wrong. Then I hear it. The coach presents the full price tag of the program, $2,000, $5,000, $10,000, etc. The client has sticker shock. Instead, the coach should have gently invited the client to get started that day with a $500 activation fee, with the first of several payments to come out 30 days later.

Don't worry, you can still ask clients to pay in full. Just do it right before you run their credit card, *not* before you solidify the sale.

MAKE IT EASY

Have you ever heard the saying, "A confused mind doesn't buy"? This is why you should only offer one payment plan. For example, if you charge $1,500 for a three-month program, you can activate the yes with a $500 activation fee, and then set up the first of two payments to be withdrawn automatically 30 days later (or whatever works best, depending on the length of your client-coach partnership). Having a system in place with one clear payment plan allows you to present yourself as a professional and shift the focus to where it should be: the client's growth.

Before you ask a client for their credit card number, ask them to confirm their name and address. This is easy for them to do. By asking them to do this first, you're preparing their brain to answer the next questions. You're also subconsciously helping the client learn that you are a good steward of their information.

You can say something like, "Let me gather some information from you as we onboard. What's your first name? I have it here as... What's your phone number? Address? Your credit card number?" As you move from one question to the next, you're easing the client into trusting you with their information.

To demonstrate that you are trustworthy, I recommend that you don't write their card information down on a piece of paper while on the call. Type it into a secure system. For my business, I use Stripe, but there are dozens of other options to choose from.

Trust-building around payments works just like the structure of the call in general. By the time you discuss money at the end of the call, you'll already have mentioned it multiple times. You'll also have talked about the value you bring many, many times, as well as the cost of staying stuck.

When you take the money from a client, you're giving them a gift. You're serving and helping them. They called on you to help them find a solution to their problems, and the exchange of money allows them to energetically take that first step forward. So be a professional and take the money. You've got this!

CELEBRATING OBJECTIONS

YOU MIGHT THINK THE TITLE OF THIS CHAPTER IS ODD. Why on earth would you celebrate objections? Aren't objections a sign that a prospective client is having doubts?

Not at all.

My belief is that there's no such thing as an objection. They don't exist if you've hosted a proper and aligned sales call. What's traditionally considered to be an objection becomes a "buying question," and I love those. In fact, I *invite* buying questions!

When a client starts asking buying questions, you should give yourself a high five and have a little dance party, because you are on the way to a yes! This person is about to enroll in your program. Don't make the mistake of getting scared or defensive when a prospective client asks a buying question. Let go, sit back, relax, and have some fun. If the client doesn't have any buying questions, it means they aren't comfortable enough to tell you what they really think.

In this chapter, I'm going to teach you how to shift your mentality and start celebrating objections. When you finish this section, I promise you'll be excited to hear your first buying question as you gently support your future client. I'll warn you, though, reading this chapter and mastering how to handle objections will *not* make up for a poorly hosted sales call that has no framework. If you don't use the Five Steps to Choice (or another aligned framework) to methodically bring a client through the sales process, you won't be successful—no matter how much you've practiced.

THE POWER OF "NO"

Before we get into specific buying questions, I want to talk about the power of the word "no." The most devastating no I've ever heard happened right after I graduated from college. I had dated the same guy for almost five years. He was practically the first guy I met when I stepped on campus. He was my first real boyfriend, my first love, my first everything. I wanted to marry him. I asked him to move back home with me after college. Then, one day, he called me.

"Michelle," he said, "I don't want to move in with you, and I don't want to marry you. In fact, I don't even want to date you anymore."

My heart broke in half. I was completely devastated. I couldn't believe how clear he was in his response. There was no equivocation, no maybe. I wept, I mourned. And then I moved on. In retrospect, that no was such a gift, because he didn't leave an energetic loop open by saying maybe.

A common post I see online from coaches is, "I'm so excited! I had a great sales calls today and the person said they might be interested in working with me!" Whenever I see this, my heart sinks, as the refrain of Jack Johnson's song *Flake* plays through my head, "maybe pretty much always means no." And sure enough, fast-forward weeks later and the coach still hasn't heard back from the client.

The problem is coaches typically don't speak up when a potential client says maybe. It's easier to try and be the nice guy and politely hang up, but that doesn't feel good. It leaves you energetically drained, and the client feels uneasy, too.

As a coach, it's your job to help the client navigate a maybe. It's your job to help bring the client to a choice. So, when a client says maybe, you can say something like, "It sounds like you aren't quite sure if this is for you. What doubts are you having as you think about our work together?"

One of my favorite open-ended responses, taught to me by an amazing sales coach named Laura Wright, is this: "On a scale of 1 to 10, how much does this feel like a fit to you?" Again, the intention is to invite an honest conversation, with the goal of supporting the client in coming to a choice before you end the call. I use a version of this almost daily, and it opens clients up to join me in thoughtful and heart-centered dialogue.

NO OBJECTIONS?

When you get no objections, it's an objection. Consider it the kiss of death. Why? Because no one plans to spend thousands of dollars and several months of their time in a coaching program and has no questions about it. When the client has no objections, it's time to get real and ask some tough questions.

You might say something like, "Great! I am so excited for us to work together. What might get in the way of achieving your goal? Is there anything you foresee that might get in the way of you stepping into and doing this work?"

See what I'm doing here? I'm inviting the client to go deeper and truly think through their next steps. Chances are that a question like this (as well as others that are provided in the bonus trainings at the end of this chapter) will help open up thoughtful and honest discussion. This will help your client make a true choice, instead of just deferring the problem.

Now, before we move on, I have to say something. If you skipped any of the previous chapters to get to this point in the book, or you turned to this chapter right away, you won't benefit from reading it. Skipping to this chapter means you're looking for a quick fix, instead of taking the time to do the inner work of sales.

There's no shortcut to connection, authenticity, and rapport. That comes from within. So if you skipped ahead to this chapter, please go back and read everything you missed. But if you've been reading this book and you've made it to this point, let's keep going.

BUYING QUESTIONS ARE OPPORTUNITIES

Okay, back to buying questions. They are absolutely amazing, and you should invite and welcome them. You should celebrate them. In fact, you should encourage the prospective client to ask *more* questions! When a client asks buying questions, it gives you the opportunity to help them make a decision. Buying questions are an indicator that you and the client are about to take a step forward.

When someone asks, "How am I going to make time for this?" they're really saying, "Help me find room in my schedule. How can I make this work?" Or if the client asks, "How am I going to afford this?" they're really saying, "Will this work for me?" These questions give you the opportunity to connect and have an honest conversation about the client's greatest fears and true desires. It's important to use your coaching skills to decode the underlying fear or question, instead of getting defensive.

WHAT OBJECTIONS TELL YOU

Coaches love to think that if they just had the magic words, they could say a certain phrase and get the client to say yes. Wouldn't it be nice to come up with a fancy sentence that would inspire a client to take out their credit card and join your program? Wouldn't it be great to find the words that would get them to step into a client-coach partnership? Unfortunately, it doesn't work that way.

If you're getting frequent objections, I invite you to return to the previous chapters of this book. Remember, when you host a proper, heart-centered sales call, you should be getting buying questions, not regular or serious objections. If you do find that you're getting objections more often than you'd like, you can also consider working with me to study the Five Steps to Choice sales framework more formally in my course, Unscripted Sales™. Together, we will learn, practice, and embody the sales conversation until it becomes second nature to you.

Think about it. Did you get to be an amazing coach by reading about coaching? Nope. It was only through hours of practice that you gained the experience, knowledge, and confidence to change your clients' lives! Practicing is the only way for the words to flow with ease.

Whether you decide to work with me or on your own, in addition to practice, you need a framework to help bring your client to a choice. You also need to understand what is going on inside of you. Figure out your money story and your thoughts and attitudes about what you charge. Show up to your calls with a clean slate. Show up 100 percent ready to support the client in front of you, and then use a framework, either the Five Steps to Choice or one from a heart-centered coach you trust. A framework helps bring the client to an aligned and embodied choice, while keeping you in command of the sales call.

UNCOVERING A CLIENT'S TRUE OBJECTION

When you get an objection of any kind, it's time to pause. Put both feet on the floor, place your hand on your heart, and be quiet for a moment.

Then ask the prospective client an open-ended question to help them feel comfortable sharing what's truly on their heart. As I mentioned earlier, one such question was taught to me when I first started selling, and it goes something like this: "On a scale of one to ten, where one is 'I want to run for the hills screaming,' and ten is 'hell yes, this program is for me,' where are you right now?" This invites the client into a safe space where they can share what is going on in their heart and mind.

The client will give an answer. If they're at six or below, it's most likely not a fit for them. However, if they're at seven or eight out of ten, say, "Great! I'd love to know seven or eight reasons why you feel this program is a fit for you."

By having the client list the potential benefits, you help the client focus on moving forward. You'll get to the truth. What is their *actual* objection? Soften, allow, and invite the client into conversation. Listen carefully to what they say. Be an investigative reporter and get to the heart of their truth.

Finding out the truth helps you figure out the issue you should address. There's no point in wasting your breath to justify the value of your program if the issue isn't really about money. You'll listen, and you'll have a real conversation about what's going on in their mind. They might initially say that money is the issue, but the truth might be that your program doesn't have what they're looking for. Or maybe they want or need to do something else before they enroll. Once you know what the real issue is, you can begin to talk about it.

Be sure to find your own words to uncover the client's true objection, but you can use this example as a guide to help you get curious and ask thoughtful questions.

THE FOUR MOST COMMON OBJECTIONS

I've hosted hundreds of sales calls, and I've found four objections to be most common:

1. "I need to talk to my spouse."

2. "I don't have time."

3. "I need to shop around."

4. "I can't afford it."

Here's how you can overcome them.

1. I Need to Talk to My Spouse

When I first started sales, I had trouble handling the spouse objection because any time I made a big decision, I asked my spouse for his input. It wasn't empowering—it felt crappy, to be honest. It also wasn't kind to my spouse because I was placing the burden of my decision onto his shoulders. So when prospective clients were on a sales call with me, guess what would happen? They'd say they had to ask their spouse.

Since communication is 55 percent nonverbal, they picked up on the fact that I assumed they would do what I did. They could hear the pause and inflection in my voice, and they could energetically sense what I was expecting. Dozens of calls later, people were still saying it.

So I did the inner work of sales. Instead of asking my spouse for permission, I began inviting him to support me. Instead of saying, "Can I go on a girls' weekend two months from now?" I said, "Hey, I'm excited to go on a girls' weekend two months from now. How can we make this happen? What kind of support do we need for the kiddos?" See the difference? Support versus permission.

I practiced this attitude shift in other way, as well. For example, instead of saying, "Honey, I think I need to make an investment in my business. What do you think?" I said, "I've decided this thing is the next best step for my business. Any idea where the funds can come from?" Notice the word "decided." A conversation about a decision I've already made is different from a conversation about whether or not I should spend the money.

It's important to approach clients gently when having this conversation. Don't just give advice; be loving and kind. Ask the client for "permission to lean in."

Once you have done the inner work to understand the spouse objection (and better yet, have used the support versus permission approach yourself), you'll have the skills to support your clients. You'll help them feel empowered. Not only on that sales call, but for the rest of their lives!

2. I Don't Have Time

I love it when prospective clients say, "I don't have time." Really, I love this objection (aka buying question) so much, because coaching is about subtracting, not adding.

When clients are in a client-coach partnership with me, they're able to find clarity about the actions they should take. It's almost like organizing their junk drawer. They get rid of things they don't need, and they find things that they thought were lost.

So, my response to the time objection is, "You don't have time? That's perfect. That's exactly why you need me." Then I can remind them of all the ways our work together is going to ease their mental and physical stress. This is truly one of the greatest benefits your client will experience with coaching. When they take the time to get right with themselves and sort through their thoughts, feelings, and desires, they can take action. They move forward boldly, saving both of you time, energy, and struggle.

3. I Need to Shop Around

Don't be afraid if a potential client says, "Great. This sounds awesome. But I need to shop around."

This is an opportunity to make it clear how knowledgeable you are. "Wonderful. Help me understand exactly what you're looking for. I can tell you where to start and what to watch out for." In the conversation that follows, you'll be able to high-light what you do differently from other coaches or service providers.

When you address the objection in this way, it becomes a benefit. You're able to restate what you do, and how amazing you are at it.

If the client insists on "shopping around" after this conversa-tion, let them. Just be sure to schedule a follow-up call for no more than three days later. This gives them the opportunity to do research, make phone calls, and do anything else they feel they need to do before they make a decision. It's important not to let more than three days go by before you speak to the client again, otherwise the energy from your initial sales call will disappear, and they're unlikely to work with you.

Shopping Around? Or Procrastination?

When a prospective client says they need to "shop around," I let them do so, but before we end the call, I ask for permission to speak freely, or "lean in" (which, as you know, I say often!). I use my gentle coaching skills to let them know that getting on a call with me might make their brain feel like they're taking action, when in fact, they may just be pushing the decision further down the road.

Next, I ask them how they'd like to be supported in making this decision. The purpose of this conversation is to make sure the client isn't procrastinating. If they truly need to interview other people or do more research, that's great. But as a coach, it's my job to help the client take embodied action. It's not my job to contribute to their procrastination.

Most often, these words shine a light on the truth. The client will realize they are, in fact, procrastinating, and they will sign up to start a client-coach partnership.

4. I Can't Afford It

As we discussed in detail in Chapter 8, the money objection is almost never about money. Remember the story I shared about my sister-in-law and how she said she couldn't afford to go to the movies, but in reality, she was *choosing* not to go? Typically, our ability to "afford" something is a choice we make, and money is a convenient scapegoat.

So the next time a prospective client says, "I can't afford it," it's most likely that they're really asking, "Will this work for me? Is this possible? Are you the right person to help me? What if I fail?" Respond to these unspoken questions first, instead of trying to convince the client of the value of your coaching.

Price Anchoring

If you're getting the "I can't afford it" objection often, my guess is that when you share the cost of your coaching, you fail to put the true value of your coaching into perspective. This practice of making clear the value of your coaching is called *price anchoring*. When you do this you're establishing a price point that customers can refer to when making decisions.

When I introduced you to heart-centered sales at the beginning of this book, we talked about how most people make decisions based on emotion and then justify them with logic. By price anchoring, you provide prospective clients with just the right amount of logic to calm their anxious brain.

A wonderful example of price anchoring comes from Laura Belgray, an amazing copywriter. She's been featured in *Forbes* magazine because she makes over a million dollars a year writing emails from her couch! It costs $10,000 to work with her for a full day, or $1,500 per hour. However, she offers an online copywriting course available a few times a year for just $499. What a steal!

Imagine if all she told you was that she has an online course that costs $499. You'd likely pass. But compared to the other prices, you understand the *value* you receive with this course.

I want to emphasize that price anchoring is not manipulative, unless you use it to deliberately trick a client, lie, or cheat, which I hope you won't do. But if you're trying to calm a client's anxious brain and give them perspective on the typical cost of programs like yours, then you're doing them an incredible service. The average consumer is unaware of the typical cost of coaching programs, nor are they used to investing in themselves. When you price anchor you're calming their anxious brain and helping them better understand the value and impact of the investment they're about to make.

WHEN IT DOESN'T GO YOUR WAY

When a prospective client you know you can help doesn't enroll, it feels awful. Despite our best efforts, sometimes the sales call just doesn't go our way. However, you can't want the transformation more than the client, as they're the ones that need to show up and do the work.

I've been doing this for so long now that if I have a sales conversation that doesn't go well, within fifteen minutes of hanging up, I can't even remember the person's name. I'm not kidding. It's not because I don't care; I care deeply. I've just energetically trained myself to cut it off. I'm a mom with three kids and can't spend time or energy carrying that around.

Nelson Mandela said, "I never lose. I either win or I learn." No matter what happens on a sales call, don't make it about you. Don't take it personally. Let it go. Quickly move on to the next thing.

SPEAK TO THE HEART, NOT THE HEAD

It's my hope that when you hear a client objection, you're now able to react with excitement and curiosity as you settle in for a thoughtful heart-to-heart conversation. Instead of getting defensive and trying to prove the value of your services, you'll get curious and use your powerful listening skills to hear beyond the surface level objection. You'll speak to their heart, rather than their head. Remember, these skills are already within you. You're already an amazing heart-centered coach! And when you host a proper sales call and methodically bring a client to a choice, the choice to work with you becomes crystal clear.

Now that we're getting excited about hosting sales calls, let's talk about ways to find clients *right now* without razzle-dazzle marketing techniques. Instead, we'll be allowing the heart-centered sales call to do the heavy lifting.

FIVE WAYS TO FIND CLIENTS

Congratulations! You've done the inner work of sales, and you've started to get a taste of how gentle and loving heart-centered sales can be. What you may not realize, though, is that by hosting sales calls properly, you start to attract clients to you like a magnet *without* formal marketing.

No, this isn't magic. But what my colleagues and I have noticed time and time again is that the internal shift and confidence that comes from knowing how to sell your coaching dramatically changes how you show up day-to-day.

When you can confidently sell your coaching, you don't hesitate to respond when a friend asks you about it. You easily strike up a conversation about coaching with someone at a mom's group, or you jump at an opportunity to speak at a networking event. Or you simply feel so excited that you post online and tell your friends what you're up to.

BUYER BEWARE

If you're a newly certified coach, you're about to see a million advertisements from "seven-figure coaches" that promise the moon. They'll share how their way of marketing helped them go from $5,000 to $500,000 in just six months.

They aren't lying, necessarily. Their methods work. From webinars to 3 or 5 day challenges, to podcast appearances and Instagram posts, there is no right or wrong way to find, sell, and deliver your coaching services.

However, there is a right and a wrong way for *you*.

If you're reading this book, you're a heart-centered coach who cares and feels deeply. Operating day-to-day in full alignment with your values and doing work that lights you up is nonnegotiable for you. And if a method or means to obtain a client doesn't feel good, it will never work for you, no matter how hard you try.

This is why it's important to be sure that any marketing course you sign up for is in alignment with your personality, values, time, and marketing budget. You want to make sure you understand exactly what the marketing method is before you make an investment to learn it. I share this because my colleagues and I have seen dozens of new coaches invest in marketing courses ranging from $10,000 to $30,000, only to discover that they didn't understand what they signed up for. If you can't find information easily, or the promises or details are vague, beware. Please wait to purchase until after you've talked with a trusted coach or mentor.

One last note on this. I feel strongly that you first learn to host heart-centered sales calls and sell your client-coach partnerships *before* you learn to market your services. This is because marketing is the act of attracting clients to you; selling is thoughtfully enrolling them in your client-coach partnerships. A marketing course may help you grow your email list, get more likes on a post, etc. However, it will not support you in hosting heart-centered sales calls. So even if you've done great marketing, you'll still be missing a vital step: sales! And what's more, the true understanding of your client's pain and struggle are discovered on the sales call itself.

FINDING CLIENTS *YOUR* WAY

Even after all my years of experience, I can still get confused about options that are available for marketing. And you really won't understand the time, energy, and financial commitment it takes to successfully market your coaching until you start.

For me, the number one way to attract new coaching clients is not through fancy marketing techniques. It's through private trainings that I offer in a small group setting.

Often, a light and easy approach is what works best to attract and sign new clients. The key (and challenge) is to discover the approach that works for you.

I can tell you that of the hundreds of coaches I've had the privilege of mentoring, the most successful ones have focused on selling a few high-ticket coaching offers each month, versus attempting to mass market their coaching. Instead of following traditional marketing practices, they follow the core methods outlined here in this chapter and build the foundation for a thriving coaching practice.

1. TAP INTO YOUR CIRCLE OF INFLUENCE

The least sexy, most underrated, yet most profitable way to sell your services as a new coach is by tapping into your circle of influence, meaning the people you already know in some capacity, even casually. These are people at your church, yoga classes, your kids' school, book club, CrossFit community, etc.

The people who already know your name are the first dozen or so that will purchase your coaching. Coaches who have sales skills and confidence in what they have to offer almost effortlessly sell their services through people they know. They do this by simply asking for and receiving referrals, and of course, rocking the sales call.

I've witnessed dozens of brand-new coaches who are over the moon excited about what they have to offer fill up their coaching programs, even group coaching programs, just by shouting it from the rooftops while in their social circles. They save time and money and help solidify their niche by learning through experience. They figure out who they want (and don't want) to work with.

If you're a coach who is also a yoga instructor, personal trainer, psychologist, reiki practitioner, massage therapist, hairdresser, esthetician, retreat leader, or in any other profession where you interact with people on a regular basis, you'll never ever have to use traditional marketing methods. I know it's hard to believe, but it's true. In fact, coaches who skip this step and immediately create a website, post on social media, and dive right into learning various marketing methods ignore the potential clients all around them. *And* it takes much longer for them to launch their coaching business.

But Don't Sell to Your Friends

Your circle of influence might start with your best friend or a family member, but please don't sell coaching to them. It's rarely a good idea to sell your services to your best friend, mother-in-law, aunt, etc. You are too close to these people, and unless you have unique circumstances, it will be difficult to be an impartial coach. Plus, selling to your friends and family all the time is just super weird and annoying.

Rather than doing this, I suggest that you ask your friends for referrals face-to-face. Who do they know that could benefit from your services? Think through this with them, and prompt them to contemplate people they know who could use coaching for their relationships, life, business, health, etc. Then give them specific instructions for how to make an introduction. For example, they can send an introductory email to the person and cc you on the message. Typically, you need to kindly ask for a referral three times before anyone will take action and make the connection. This isn't personal and asking more than once doesn't mean you're bothering them. People are just busy, and unless prompted, they will put it off.

Success Is a Choice

My colleagues and I are continually baffled by coaches who fail to make offers and sell coaching through their circle of influence. On the other hand, we've also been inspired by new coaches that sell $2,000, $5,000, and even $10,000 client-coach partnerships while they're still in coach training! We ponder, study, and contemplate why some coaches are successful and why others struggle to even make a single offer to folks through their circle of influence, given the same training.

Our conclusion: It's not that certain coaches have more confidence or better sales skills than others. While this is important, it's not the reason for their success. The most successful coaches have *decided* to be coaches and sell their services. They've gotten over their own thoughts and misnomers that they're selling themselves. Instead, they focus on the product and the results, and have real conversations with people, rather than hiding behind marketing.

I hope you're reading this book while still in coach training, or after recently graduating from your program, as this is the ideal time to share your new role with friends and family. But if not, don't worry. It's never too late to tap into your circle of influence.

Getting Started: The CEO Challenge

I invite you to participate in the Connect, Engage, and Offer (CEO) Challenge. An amazing coach and colleague of mine, Carly Clark Zimmer, first introduced this idea within the BodyMind Coaching program. It's simple: reach out to two people per day for twenty days, for a total of forty people. Simply share information about your work, ask for a referral, or invite people to a sales call. This should take you no more than fifteen minutes a day, and after the twenty days, it will become a part of your daily routine. The very first time I tried this, I was invited to speak to a group of thirteen new coaches in training, booked two sales calls, and even landed two amazing guests for my podcast! The simplicity and success of this challenge is incredible!

With everything you do in sales and marketing, you'll want to track what you do and measure your results. A downloadable spreadsheet is available in the online resource section of this book to track your progress during the CEO Challenge.

At first, it will feel like you've asked one hundred people for referrals, but when you look at your spreadsheet, you'll realize it wasn't that many. Create a routine for yourself so that you spend fifteen minutes reaching out to your circle of influence daily, connecting and asking, "Who do you know that could use help with [insert problem that needs to be solved]?"

2. SELL TO EXISTING CLIENTS (IF YOU HAVE 'EM)

As I stated earlier, if you're a coach and yoga instructor, massage therapist, sex educator, reiki practitioner, personal trainer, or in another profession where you see clients on a regular basis, you're all set. You don't need to read any more of this chapter. In fact, you can stop after this section.

You don't have to concern yourself with marketing, because you have all you need to quickly grow a thriving coaching practice. You get to skip traditional marketing practices and simply fall in love with your coaching offer. You get to have heart-centered sales conversations! If this is you, your focus right now and for the foreseeable future should be exclusively on learning the sales conversation, loving your offer, and selling the heck out of it.

Get Out of Your Own Way

If you have existing service-based clients, you have a gold mine right in front of you! Don't fall into the trap of thinking that these clients are not "ideal" coaching clients. Oftentimes, new coaches ignore the clients right in front of them because they've yet to do the inner work of sales, and they're not confident about all they have to offer.

Some of your existing clients will say no, and that's okay. About 20 percent of them will say yes. While not everyone will want or need a coach, if you're selling client-coach partnerships for thousands of dollars, you only need one or two new clients per month to change your income dramatically. You have a unique opportunity because service-based clients walk through your door every day.

The in-person sales conversation with these clients is key, as traditional ways of selling your services won't be as effective. Remember, you built your existing business on referrals, and your coaching practice is no different. If clients are coming to you on a regular basis for any type of service, I guarantee you a percentage of those clients will be interested in your coaching offer.

Getting Started: Change How Clients See You

First, tell every client that comes into your office or studio that in addition to your hands-on work, you now also offer coaching. You can now help them meet their life, health, and wellness goals on a deeper level.

Second, be sure to track your progress. This is important because you may feel like you've told everyone, but really, you've only told five people. Mark somewhere in your database or client paperwork each time you share your offer with someone. And once you finish telling everyone, celebrate! Post online or take yourself out to lunch. This second step is a really big deal, and when you complete it, you should feel amazing.

Third, after you share that you're a coach, ask clients if they'd be interested in learning more about coaching. When they say, "Heck yes," be ready to schedule a time to talk with them in person or via video chat. In my experience, I've found that 20 percent of clientele will respond with a yes. And don't be discouraged by those that don't. Remember, it's your job to present the opportunity for them to learn more, not to make judgments in your head about what the client desires. And for those clients that say, "No, thank you" ask them who they know that might be interested in this amazing transformative work. People love to be helpful, which makes this a win-win!

Finally, use the amazing heart-centered coaching skills you've learned in this book, along with my Five Steps to Choice sales framework (or other aligned method), to have an empowered conversation with your client and invite them to join you in a client-coach partnership. By being brave and making offers, you help your clients to step up and get the support they need to live healthier, happier lives.

3. OFFER PRIVATE SMALL GROUP WORKSHOPS

Offering free or paid private workshops to small groups such as moms' groups, fitness groups, book clubs, entrepreneurial groups, etc. is an amazing way to get in front of clients, show off your coaching skills, and serve small groups or organizations. Unlike posting online and hoping people sign up, when you host a private training for a group or organization, you have a built-in audience with an immediate high level of trust. I'm going to share what's worked for me but having someone within a group as a sponsor for your talk is ideal. That way, they can advertise on your behalf so people will gain interest and attend your workshop.

What Worked for Me

Again, offering private training in small group settings has been the number one way I've attracted new coaching clients. Most coaches form private online groups to support each other during and after their coach certification training, and I go into these groups (by private invitation) to offer customized training on sales. Typically, after each training, multiple people reach out and say they want to work with me! This is another win-win, because it's light and easy for me, and supports the coaching cohort tremendously.

Imposter Syndrome is Real
(But Don't Let It Stop You)

Imposter syndrome is loosely defined as doubting your abilities and feeling like a fraud. It disproportionately affects high-achieving people, who find it difficult to accept their accomplishments.[7]

Coaches at all levels experience feelings of being a fraud or not being good enough. If you're not sure what to offer in a private training, think back to your own coach training. What exercise or tool did you love most? Was it an exercise on boundaries, or perhaps time management? If you have a favorite exercise, you don't need to completely reinvent the wheel.

For example, if you're a health coach and participated in a mindful eating workshop in the past, you can simply create something similar, but with your own unique spin! Be sure to give credit to the author or coach that first introduced you to the challenge or exercise and get written permission if you use copyrighted materials. But *do not* let imposter syndrome stop you! You have every right to offer training on a topic that another person has already done. There is only one YOU, and your version will be brilliant!

Getting Started: Making Connections

Refer back to the CEO Challenge at the beginning of the chapter. During your fifteen minutes of daily outreach and engagement, ask individuals what groups or organizations they

7   Ruchika Tulshyan and Jodi-Ann Burey, "Stop Telling Women They Have Imposter Syndrome," Harvard Business Review, February 11, 2021, https://hbr. org/2021/02/stop-telling-women-they-have-imposter-syndrome.

belong to. Then ask if the company, organization, or group would be interested in an in-person or online training. Not everyone will say yes, but in my experience, about one person per week will be very excited and welcome you in to host a free (or paid) training.

Pro Tip

Create your own sign-up page for the event. Ask the host to share the sign-up page, so you can send reminders to participants. This is a win-win, as the host doesn't have to do the hard work of gathering email addresses, and you'll automatically have a list of prospects.

---

4. GET SOCIAL

A common way to launch a coaching practice is by creating a private online group, using a platform such as Facebook. It's free, you can start a group immediately, and it can give you the sense of security you need to share your coaching with others.

An aligned and well-run group on Facebook or another social platform can quickly launch you into a booked-out coaching practice. Invite your circle of influence and watch as your Facebook group supports and grows your community.

Before you dive into an online group, be sure you've sold several three-, six-, or twelve-month client-coach partnerships through your circle of influence. That way, as you start your group you'll have a niche and testimonials to share, and you can coach and speak from experience.

Create a Plan

Managing a social media group takes daily work, engagement, thought, and lots of time! If you don't manage your time properly and have a plan for your posts, engagement, and how to promote your coaching offers (such as inviting people to calls), you will quickly feel drained with few or no results.

Also, if you haven't taken the time to learn how to host a properly aligned, heart-centered sales call, your online group will not be successful. When you lack confidence with sales calls, it shows energetically in your posts and client interactions. If you haven't spoken with real people on sales calls, it also creates a gap in your marketing, because you haven't learned your clients' true pain points.

Lastly, online groups can attract "looky loos," or folks who have no intention of buying. Ever. This is why having a plan to get people from your group onto a sales call is so important. Nurturing an audience is great, but selling your coaching is much better.

The key takeaway here is to have a plan to sell your coaching. Don't just show up and hope for the best.

Getting Started: Your First Online Group

Before you feel 100 percent ready, create a private online group, but don't invite anyone yet. By waiting to let people into your group, it allows you to get comfortable with the features the platform has to offer, like videos, surveys, admission questions, etc. Take some time to observe an existing group you love and notice what you like and don't like. Which posts are getting engagement and which posts are falling flat?

Also, think of how you want to show up regularly in the group. A weekly live video? A roundtable? Q&A? The possibilities are endless. After you've completed the CEO Challenge and sold to your first handful of clients, you can open up your group and start flexing your coaching muscles!

Pro Tip

Include two to three posts each week that specifically invite group members to a one-on-one private sales call with you. Do not skip this step. Think of creative and playful ways to do this. It may take three to six months before you start booking calls from this method, but it's important that you don't just "hang out" and offer advice in your private online group.

5. HOST A 3 OR 5 DAY CHALLENGE

After you've sold about a dozen three-, six-, or twelve-month client-coach partnerships, you're confident in your coaching, and your online group has gained traction, a 3 or 5 day challenge might be your next step!

Here's how challenges *typically* work: As a coach, you will offer value on a particular topic for say, five days, for one hour each day. The first two days will be purely value-based, with a brief tease or mention of how you can partner with clients. Then on the fourth and fifth days, you'll invite the clients to a sales call to see if they're aligned to work with you one-on-one or in your group program. Of course, there are dozens of ways to host a challenge, so figuring out what works for you and your audience is key!

You can also modify this challenge and do a one-day workshop, which is a great way to see what will resonate with your ideal clientele.

The Metrics

You want to understand and measure the appropriate metrics when running a challenge. I often counsel coaches who are upset because they only enrolled a few people after hosting a challenge. However, when I break down the average attendance and conversion rates, they are pleasantly surprised.

Be sure to download this chapter's resource guide to help support you when you're ready to host your own challenge.

Getting Started: Release the Outcome

A mentor once told me to host a challenge in my online group without any expectations of success. I loved this idea! The planning of a 3 or 5 day challenge is lots of work, and when you're focusing on the logistics of the event, signing clients, and delivering your program, it's just too much to have expectations.

Take it one step at a time, and simply offer your 3 or 5 day challenge to find out if it resonates with the group. Emails (reminders, teasers for each day, follow-ups, and sales sequences) are a large part of the work here. So skip all of that at first, and just get playful and curious by inviting a small number of people to join your first live challenge.

Pro Tip

During a 3 or 5 day challenge, you'll be tempted to share the price of your coaching and all the other details in an attempt to enroll people into your programs. This is a big mistake. Only the most elite coaches in our industry are able to do this successfully, but it isn't time for you to do this yet. For now, simply invite people to a coaching call. If they want to gain more clarity and figure out their next steps, use your heart-centered sales skills to onboard them as new clients.

THE TIME IS NOW

There are clients all around you right now! Open your mind and heart and invite in new clients today. Remember, you will find and sign your first coaching clients through your circle of influence. You want to sell three-, six-, or twelve-month client-coach partnerships so you'll be in business immediately, rather than selling one-off sessions.

Your first clients will provide you with the testimonials and confidence to start expanding your network, claim your niche, and solidify your coaching offer that will light you up from the inside out! Ideally, after a year or more of coaching, you'll be ready to expand beyond your circle of influence.

Before you dive into and invest in marketing your coaching in a specific way, be sure to think through everything involved (time, money, etc.). Make sure to research, observe, and experience the various ways your peers sell their coaching before you invest in a program. Rather than consulting a marketing expert, take marketing advice from seasoned coaches who sell the same or similar services. When in doubt, ask a trusted mentor before investing in a marketing program.

And finally, follow your alignment. If something feels scary or new, that's okay. But if a marketing effort feels out of alignment with you and your values, stop. There are hundreds of ways to market and sell your coaching, and for heart-centered coaches, alignment and integrity must be front and center.

To download the most up-to-date version of this chapter plus additional ways to find coaching clients, spreadsheets to track your progress, and links to trusted resources, go to: www.michellerockwood.com/joyful.

CONCLUSION

SALES CAN BE INCREDIBLE, HEART-CENTERED, AND life-affirming. We should celebrate sales for its ability to create a connection with a client and helping them make a life-changing decision they've never dreamed of before.

I'm sure it's obvious by now how much I love sales. Most days it doesn't even feel like a job! I fall into a rhythm, and I show up fully embodied to sales calls. Over time, I've found that clients (the right clients) are naturally drawn to me.

My hope is that this book has given you an inspirational message, and that it's completely transformed the way you view sales. My dream is that every new coach is handed this book upon enrollment in their coach certification program or upon graduation. This would collectively raise the bar in our profession and change the face of sales forever. I want every coach to approach sales with a new perspective, and for old thought patterns and habits to be replaced with new ones. I hope all coaches will see what sales should look like, and that you realize the power and impact it can have in your life and in the lives of your clients.

Let's recap the key points we talked about in each chapter:

- **Chapter 1:** I taught you how to turn your coaching into a high-ticket offer. You become the client's partner. Offer client-coach partnerships, and don't sell single sessions.

- **Chapter 2:** We talked about the differences between masculine and feminine sales energies and why the feminine style of sales works when selling coaching programs. You don't chase... you receive!

- **Chapter 3:** We talked about how to set yourself up for success. Host forty-five-minute calls, set clear boundaries, and follow the Five Golden Rules.

- **Chapter 4:** We talked about the goal of the sales call. It's not to get the prospective client to say yes; it's uncovering the true transformation the client is seeking and opening the door to working on that transformation. Even if it's *without you*.

- **Chapter 5:** We talked about building rapport to stop the sales yuck. Create deep, meaningful, visceral, energetic connections with others and watch the yeses start rolling in!

- **Chapter 6:** We learned that prospective clients will tell lies. They may not do this intentionally; it could just be that they don't understand their true struggles. Ask thoughtful questions to help them uncover their real problem and help them understand the cost of inaction.

- **Chapter 7:** We took the next step and talked about helping clients understand their true desire. Lead them through embodiment exercises to bring them to their heart center, because decisions are made by the body, not the brain.

- **Chapter 8:** We learned how to get our hands out of other people's pockets. What someone can or can't afford is none of our business, and we aren't to make judgements based on appearance. Your job is to present the opportunity, and then let the client decide if they can afford it.

- **Chapter 9:** We talked about the importance of taking the money. You do this by beginning the partnership with an activation fee, and then continue to take the money through a monthly automatic payment. This makes payments easy for the client, and they won't have to reenroll in the decision over and over again.

- **Chapter 10:** We learned how to view objections in a different way. Instead of being afraid of them, they should be celebrated! Objections become buying questions that give you the opportunity to help the client make their choice.

- **Chapter 11:** We learned five things you can do *right now* to tap into your network and sell your coaching.

If you feel you're able to take away what you've learned here and dive into heart-centered sales, that's wonderful. But if you want more help, or want to go deeper, this is where I invite you to join my program. I'd love to help you reach the next level of success by teaching you my Unscripted Sales Method, the Five Steps to Choice. This is the key on which my business turns, and how I've helped hundreds of coaches sell millions of dollars in coaching, most before they even graduated from their coach certification program. When you join my program, we'll begin a coaching partnership, and you'll learn how to sell joyfully, with your full heart and soul.

Whether you choose to work with me or not, you do need to trust that you have everything within you to be successful in sales. You have heart and truly care about your clients. You are fully capable, amazing, and perfect just the way you are. Use the principles and philosophy contained within this book to shape the sales framework that will work best for you, but don't cling to it as a how-to manual. Create a plan, learn it, and practice it. Once you do this, you're ready to do the work of sales and coaching.

Knowing what you know now, why would you ever go back to the old sell, sell, sell mentality? You can act from your heart center and be wildly profitable, while working with fewer clients and making more money. You can sell with full integrity, in a way that's in alignment with your values.

Additional Resources

If you've found this book to be beneficial, please share it with the leaders of your coach training program, professional organizations, and coaching peers who want to learn how to sell from their heart center. And I'd love to help you reach the next level of success by teaching you my Unscripted Sales Method™, the Five Steps to Choice. To learn more about how you can work with me, visit www.michellerockwood.com or email info@michellerockwood.com.

And to access trusted resources mentioned throughout this book visit www.michellerockwood.com/joyful.

ACKNOWLEDGMENTS

I'D LIKE TO THANK MY AMAZING COACH AND MENTOR, Laura Wieck, who overheard me talking at a party years ago. I was sharing the story of how I raised one million dollars over lunch for charity, and she quickly hired me to lead her sales team. We both remember that day vividly, and on that day my journey into heart-centered sales began. I'm forever grateful to her and the hundreds of coaches that have said yes to this method of selling, and have opened their hearts, minds, and businesses to a new way of working.

I'd also like to acknowledge Melissa Kelley and Melanie Grimm, two amazing coaches who first shared their sales calls with me years ago. They got me hooked on studying and perfecting the sales call process. I'd like to also thank Melissa Grossman, an amazing colleague and friend who isn't afraid of hard work and who will kick your butt if you ever mess with her man in a bar!

And of course, thanks to another amazing coach and mentor, Laura Wright, whose brilliance and confidence inspire me daily. I'd also like to thank my big brother, Lucas Rockwood, who told me to write this book, and whose mentorship and friendship I cherish deeply. And, of course, thank you to my amazing parents, Mike and Yvonne Rockwood.

Thank you to my husband, Ryan, for loving and supporting the heck out of me, and living a life of humility and integrity. And thanks to my three boys who inspire me to work smarter, and always help me remember the bigger vision our family has for our lives.

And finally, to my editor, Geneva Ross, for all the laughter and love that went into every edit, modification, and last-minute addition. I, and heart-centered coaches everywhere, are forever grateful to you.

ABOUT THE AUTHOR

Michelle Rockwood has sold real estate in one of the world's wealthiest communities, slept on a dirt floor in West Africa while serving in the US Peace Corps, and once raised a million dollars for charity over a single lunch. Now a personal coach and widely recognized sales expert, Michelle has helped hundreds of heart-centered coaches discover sales methods that feel fantastic, transforming their businesses and their lives.

Michelle is the founder of Unscripted Sales™, a consulting firm for sales teams and coaching certification companies of all sizes. She specializes in helping coach training companies teach their clients (coaches in training) how to create client-coach partnerships and sell their coaching.

After personally hosting more than four hundred sales conversations and shifting entire sales teams into life-changing revenues, Michelle wrote *Joyful Selling* to share her knowledge with all the loving, heart-centered coaches our world so desperately needs.

Michelle resides in Colorado with her husband Ryan and three boys, Julian, Miles, and Silas, and her fur babies, Tigo and Ruby.

Lightning Source UK Ltd.
Milton Keynes UK
UKHW041609020323